WHAT IS FAITH?

The Why God Why Series

WHAT
IS
FAITH?

Helen Glowacki

Novels by Helen Glowacki

When God Broke Grandma's Heart
When God Took Grandma Home
When Grandma Chased the Spirits
The Granddaughter and the Monkey Swing
The Story of God's Plan of Salvation
Abiding Faith, Hidden Treasure
And Then They Asked God
Caleb's Testimony

Why God Why Series by Helen Glowacki

To What Purpose?
Why God Why?
Why Trust Scripture?
Life after Death And The Coming Tribulation
What Does God Want Me To Do RIGHT NOW?
Do Our Little Sins *Really* Count?
What Do Angels Do?
What is Faith?
Satan's Gift of Fear

Other non-fiction Books by Helen Glowacki

Politically Incorrect: When Enough is Enough
Overcoming Depression: How to be Happy
What No One Is Telling You about Addictions

****

Authors Website: www.helenglowacki.com

Face book: http://www.facebook.com/pages/The-Grandmother-Series/155300907853909?ref=ts and also
http://www.facebook.com/pages/Helenglowacki/

The Why God Why Series

WHAT
IS
FAITH?

Helen Glowacki

For more information or to purchase additional copies of this book email helen@helenglowacki.com or visit her website @ www.helenglowacki.com or Amazon.com.

MISSION STATEMENT

To Serve

God

With All Our Strength

And

All Our Heart

Helen Glowacki

NOTE TO THE READER

The King James Version (KJV) of the Bible, which is public domain in the United States, is used throughout all the books written by this author. For further study, the author recommends the New King James Version (NKJV) of the Bible as easier reading and less usage of the old world language while remaining true to the original text.

The non-fiction books by Helen Glowacki represent the opinion, research, religious beliefs and scriptural interpretations of the author and are not meant to be used in lieu of the advice of ministerial, theological, medical or psychological experts.

The novels by Helen Glowacki are works of fiction. While some events in these novels reflect the expertise and support of those in particular vocations, references to real people, events, organizations, or locales are intended only to provide a sense of authenticity, and are used fictitiously. Characters, incidents and dialogue are drawn from the author's imagination and are not to be construed as real. Any resemblance to actual persons, living or dead is entirely coincidental.

<u>ACKNOWLEDGEMENTS</u>

Special thanks to my husband Wally who provided so much support to my work and made my computer behave. Thanks to my children and grandchildren for the constancy of their love and encouragement, and to Reverend Herold Ambroise for his fervent prayers on my behalf.

Special thanks to Richard Levinson for providing the first opportunity through which I could develop my writing skills. I will never forget that kindness.

Thanks to my brothers and sisters and ministers in faith who give so freely of their love and prayers, and to my Face book friends who also pray for me and support this ministry.

My thanks to Katharina Leipp of Muhlaker, Germany for her incredible friendship and support, and for translating *Caleb's Testimony,* and the tabletop version of *The Story of God's Plan of Salvation* and many of my articles, into the German language.

Thanks to Juan Capurro for translating *The Story of God's Plan of Salvation* into the Spanish language. This was such a special gift!

Thanks also to Darren Robinson for his meticulous assembly of the cover and to Daniel Patrick Landolfi for maintaining the website.

But most of all, my heartfelt, humble thanks to our Heavenly Father for His inspiration, guiding hand, protection, and never-ending love.

May this work bring joy to His heart and help find that last soul!

"One thing have I

desired of the Lord,

that I will seek after;

that I may dwell

in the house of the Lord

all the days of my life,

to behold the beauty of the Lord,

and to enquire in his temple."

Psalm 27: 4

MESSAGE FROM THE AUTHOR

Scripture tells us that faith is the substance of things hoped for, the evidence of things not seen. But, because we so easily lose patience in waiting for our hopes to be realized, and have difficulty recognizing the evidence of what is touched or seen, faith will vary in degree not only from person to person, but day by day. Scripture also tells us that without faith we will not withstand the evil of the end times. Thus our dilemma is how to build our faith despite our impatience and our need for immediate proof. Adding to this problem is the fact that Satan and his fallen angels work day and night to plant doubt, confusion and complacency into our minds about what little faith we can muster. We wonder then how we are to build our faith and how can we escape the destruction of faith which Satan wreaks upon the children of God. Satan works to keep us from trusting God's instruction and protection.

Scripture also teaches us that we may lack the armour with which to fight Satan's assault because we do not understand why Satan has power, why we suffer under his assaults, why we must follow God's statutes, or what the demanding challenges of the end times really means to us. When we have little knowledge about these matters it is difficult to grasp why faith grows from trusting the omnipotence of God and believing that He is a caring Heavenly Father who loves and protects us. Nor do we understand that the stronger our faith in God, the more we pray in thankfulness rather than need; the more we accept God's decisions for our life, and the less fear and anxiety we experience.

The words in Hosea 4:6 tell us: *"My people are destroyed for lack of knowledge....."* which explains that faith requires an understanding of the Plan of Salvation which God instituted for our benefit. Hosea 4:6 goes on to say:...*"because thou hast rejected knowledge, I will also reject thee....."*. These words warn that if we ignore the opportunity God provides for us to learn His words, understand His Plan, and accept the righteousness under which He must labour, we may be rejected when Christ returns just as the five foolish virgins were rejected. Few understand that God has put into place the boundaries in which He works and under which we must work. Nor do they know that even Christ asked if He would find faith in those He loves when He returns.

We often think of the word faith as something which is associated with God, but we actually use faith everyday for everyday purposes. For instance, when we visit a doctor and he prescribes an antibiotic we have faith not only in the doctor's knowledge about what we require, but also that the medicine will do what it is supposed to do. When we go to a restaurant and order a meal, we have faith that it will be tasty and safe to eat. When we send our children to school, we have faith that they will be taught what they need to know. We use faith everyday and rarely think about measuring it. It is only when what we have believed will occur *fails* to occur, that we begin to question that belief. We begin to feel that we can no longer trust what we once did trust. Therefore we can lose our faith very quickly.

Faith in God however, differs because we are asked us to hold onto our faith even when God does not do what we expect Him to do. We are asked to believe that all things work for the good of those who love the Lord, therefore whatever occurs is under God's control and meant for our good even when we cannot see that good. Therefore, having faith in God requires practice. It requires a certain mindset which has made the decision to trust God. Consciously deciding to employ our faith during the difficult times when we cannot see God's reasons, almost always guarantees that God will provide us with what is termed a "miracle of faith" to teach us that He is indeed to be trusted.

As we reach out to God despite our circumstances, letting Him know that we have simply consciously "decided" to trust Him, He lets us know that He is always there for us. In fact, the many little things which we'd once viewed as "coincidence" is suddenly seen as God's work in our life. As our faith grows, our prayers become more thankful and our concerns move from anxiety to a calm and patient expectation that we will accept and be thankful for our circumstances.

But unlike the ease with which we can move our faith in one laundry product to another, our faith in God must remain with Him alone. Without knowledge of *why* we need to develop faith or *why* it will be tested, it is difficult to retain the faith/belief that God is in control of *all* things and always has our best interest at heart. Nor will we understand why it is important to Satan to separate us from God and why he has the power and the desire to use our selfish, impatient human nature to do so. However God knows all these things and therefore encourages us throughout all of scripture to *know* Him; to learn of Him; to understand what His goals are for us, and why there are forces working against His Plan of Salvation. Without this knowledge, our quest for faith is more challenging, and our faith cannot increase. Neither can it withstand the onslaught it will receive. Nevertheless, scripture tells us that faith can grow so strong that it can "move mountains".

But when our faith is weak we find that our lives are a constant repeat of every anxiety we have ever felt. We find ourselves re-visiting some of the same problems over and over again. Neither can we seem to break the destructive patterns we see operating in our lives. Scripture teaches us that if we do take that first leap of faith, we will find the means with which we can interrupt the patterns which seem to plague us. Such a leap of faith requires that we ask God to help us and believe that He will. Thus, having faith is important and because of its importance, scripture teaches us about faith and about the power it contains.

In Matthew 8:5-13 we read that one day when Jesus entered into the town of Capernaum, a soldier approached Him and requested that He heal the soldiers servant. Jesus offered to go to the soldiers home to provide this healing, but the soldier said that he was not worthy to have Jesus come under his roof and told Jesus that if He would simply speak a word of healing, it would be done. Jesus marveled at the strong faith which this man exhibited and said *"Go thy way; and **as thou hast believed, so be it done** unto thee".* And the soldier's servant was healed in that same hour.

Another account of the power of faith is found in Matthew 17:14-20 which describes a time when Christ was asked to heal a man's son because the disciples of Christ had been unable to do so. When Christ performed the healing, his disciples asked him why they were unsuccessful in their attempt to heal this boy and Christ answered: *"**Because of your unbelief:** for verily I say unto you, **If ye have faith** as the grain of a mustard seed, ye shall say unto this mountain, Remove hence to yonder place; and it shall remove; and **nothing shall be impossible unto you**".* Similarly in Luke 17:5-6 we read: *"And the apostles said unto the Lord, **Increase our faith**. And the Lord said, If ye had faith as a grain of mustard seed, ye might say unto this sycamine tree, Be thou plucked up by the root, and be thou planted in the sea; and it should obey you."*

These verses and many others throughout scripture teach us about the power of faith. Others teach us how we can increase our faith. Acts 14:27 tells us: *"And when they....had gathered the church together, they **rehearsed all that God had done with them, and how he had opened the door of faith.....**"* This verse tells us that we must share (*rehearse*) the many things we have learned (*God had done*) about our belief system so that all the pieces of God's Plan of Salvation can take shape not only in our minds but in our hearts. Our desire to learn allows God to plant the seed of faith in our heart (*open the door of faith*) which we must then nurture. As we learn of God and His loving compassion, we begin to see the kind of person God wants us to be. Galatians 5:22-23 tells us that in everything we do and think we are to exercise *"love, joy, peace, patience, kindness, goodness, faithfulness, gentleness and self-control".*

It is through God's own words in scripture that we can learn all we need to know about our Heavenly Father and why He is trying to mold us into a people with these attributes. In fact, one particular phrase in scripture is repeated so often that we easily recognize the importance of its message which tells us that we must learn God's Plan of Salvation and **through this knowledge**, must and can increase our faith. This phrase speaks about the need for us to *"hear"* the word of God by being with believers who discuss or preach the truths God wants us to learn. Some examples of this message can be found in 2 Chronicles 15:2, Ezekiel 3:27, Revelation 2:7, 11, 17, 29, Revelation 3:6, 13, 22, and in Revelation 22:17. They all suggest that one must *"come"* to where God's word is taught and then *"hear"* what the Spirit of God wants to bring them. For example, Revelation 3:6, 13, and 22 repeat the words: *"He that hath an ear, **let him hear** what the Spirit sayeth unto the churches......"*. Thus what God is telling us is that as we increase our understanding of His plan for our lives and future, our faith will grow. We will begin to **understand the magnitude of why we were born and to what end we must strive.** We will understand the process required for God to separate good from evil for all eternity.

While many simply disregard scripture, and others believe its words are mystical allegories impossible to apply, there are many more who *desire* to understand scripture so they can make an **informed** decision about whether or not they will choose to use its directives to guide their lives. Those who do trust scripture believe, as I do, that scripture is the word of God given to develop the Bride of Christ and the children of God for His new kingdom. **It is important that we take from scripture those things which teach us about our future and how we can attain the understanding we require.** Scripture warns that it is through our *lack* of understanding that many will lose their soul salvation. Therefore, whether allegory or fact, or whether couched in a mystery which is unveiled as we gain a better understanding of God's Plan of Salvation, God's asks us to trust Him and tells us that our trust will be greatly enhanced and deeply rooted *when we learn His words.*

Everything we learn from scripture helps us through the growth process we undergo here on earth; it helps us appreciate the plan

God has put into place to bring us a new world free of all evil, thus free of sorrow. As we read scripture and begin to understand it's words we develop the ability to recognize the immensity of God's plan for our future and the love and patience with which He draws us. It is a process which helps us grow into a more selfless person cognizant of the fact that each of us will one day make, consciously or unconsciously, the ever important decision to follow Gods statutes or allow ourselves to remain complacent. It is our personal decision and not one that anyone else can make for us.

This book will explain in simple language much of what God teaches through scripture. It has been developed for those who have limited time for investigating and compiling the many nuances of the Holy Bible. It is a book which provides short, concise explanations of the many and various parts of God's Plan of Salvation.

I hope that you will enjoy this little book and that you will share what you learn with others. May God open your understanding of His words and may He bless you and keep you always.

Helen Glowacki

TABLE OF CONTENTS

" . . . ..above all

taking the shield

of faith,

with which you can

quench

all the flaming darts

of the evil one."

Ephesians 6:16

> "For we wrestle not against flesh and blood, but against principalities, against powers, against the rulers of the darkness of this world, against spiritual wickedness in high places."
> Ephesians 6:12

Chapter One

THE RULE OF RIGHTEOUSNESS

Many have fallen into the dangerous complacency of believing that they have "enough" understanding about God to provide them with access to Heaven. Others believe that because they know that God has instituted a Plan of Salvation which provides grace, they do not have to do any more to be a part of God's new kingdom. Yet, when we read the parable of the five wise and the five foolish virgins in Matthew 25:1-13, it clearly points out that these assumptions are dangerous. As we examine this parable we learn that all ten virgins were faithful. All ten believed that Christ would come for them, all were dutifully waiting for Him, and all fully expected to go with Him when He returned.

When we ask ourselves *why* the five foolish virgins were left behind and what made them different than the five wise virgins, we learn that the five foolish virgins had not filled their lamps with oil. Thus, at the last minute they had to obtain the oil they needed and while they were engaged in this effort, the Lord came and took those who were ready; those who had kept their lamps full. We then read that when the five foolish virgins returned with their lamps filled once again, it was too late...the Lord had left without them. The door had closed to them and they realized that they had been left behind. Though they begged Christ to open the door for them, He did not, and they were shocked to find that they would not be taken.

When scripture refers to the oil required to keep a lamp lit it is often teaching us to keep our path well lit by utilizing the "light" of understanding. This light comes through Christ whose life of testimony and sacrificial death was the beacon which offered a path by which mankind could be brought out of the darkness of this world and the sin in it. Therefore what we learn from the words in this parable is that without constantly filling our hearts and minds with the word of God, and our soul with the forgiveness Christ offers, we may not find our way through the darkness of evil which will prevent us from becoming those who God will bring into His new kingdom.

Supporting this deduction are the verses in scripture which explain that many **will not be taken when Christ returns because of a "lack of knowledge".** (Hosea 4:6)   This verse in Hosea, combined with the verses we read in the parable of the five wise and five foolish virgins are a warning to us.   They tell us that we must prepare our soul by increasing our knowledge of scripture so that we *can* satisfy the pre-requisites of God's righteousness. Knowledge of God's plan allows us to understand *why* we need the "light" of Christ's sacrifice by replenishing the "oil" of God's words. Christ's sacrifice allows the forgiveness of our sins but it is God's words which teach us its value and its rules of engagement.

Sadly, few of us ask ourselves if we truly "know" God; if we know *what* He plans, *what* He offers, and *what* pre-requisites there may be for a future with Him. Many are so complacent or so sure that they are "okay" in their current state, that they don't investigate what God is offering. Thus, few ask how they can obtain the forgiveness of their sins *worthily.* Few consider that we should be so in love with our Heavenly Father and the Bridegroom of our soul that we **constantly** seek to learn of Them, and that we **hunger** to listen to what They tell us through scripture, that we **desire** to please Them, and thus **work** every day to replenish the fragrant oil of Their instruction. To accomplish this we must try to understand what God is; what He wants, and what He offers before we dismiss the entire concept of "faith" or find fault with parts of scripture.

We must also learn what the "righteousness" of God actually means so we can unravel some of the mysteries attached to the requirements God has laid out for us. This helps us understand how to keep our "passports" to heaven up-to-date. If we do not want to be left behind for "lack of knowledge", we must begin to learn what God seeks in those He will choose for His new kingdom. We need to know **what** is required and **why** it is required so we can make an informed decision about whether or not we are willing to labour for that prize.

God's righteousness is fascinating to study. *All* things are possible to our Heavenly Father, the Creator of everything; the One who is omnipresent and omnipotent. Yet God placed upon *Himself* the single limitation that as He works to create a world without evil He would do so under the rule of righteousness. When we question why God would take on this added burden, we begin to see an incredible picture of the physics of this world and of the the world which God is preparing for our future.

Most of us acknowledge that our current world is comprised of opposites which God put into place as a part of the physics of the universe. These rules of physics require our universe to function *in harmony* with all its various components. If such balances had not been put into place, what would stop the chaos of a system which did not require for instance the laws of gravity to control the moon's power over the ebb and flow of our oceans? How would light chase away darkness? How would love offset the horror of evil? Where would a ball go if it did not come back down after throwing it as high as we could?

God chose to create and bring His Plan of Salvation to fruition *only* in and through complete and absolute righteousness. As we ponder this phenomenon we might also examine the word "unrighteousness" which is the opposite of the word "righteousness". Unrighteousness is chaos and it follows no rules or regulations. It has no boundaries. Scripture teaches us that God chose to act only in righteousness so that **all evil and all hate** (unrighteousness) **could be removed forever and could have no claim on His new kingdom.**

What this means to us is that no matter how "nice" or "good" we are, **there** *are* **rules**...absolute rules under His rule of righteousness...which God has chosen to follow as He labours to develop us into a special people for the new kingdom. Since the new kingdom will be free of sin, free of all unrighteousness, we cannot bring with us any unrighteousness which we harbour even in the hidden recesses of our heart. This is why God offers us the forgiveness of sin and wants us to learn what sin and unrighteousness is in His perfect world.

When we are willing to learn and strive to meet these pre-requisites, God offers us His blessings. This includes ...among many things..... the forgiveness of sin, the gift of the Holy Spirit, and the offer to become the Bride of Christ. We may all long to become a resident of the new Heaven and Earth, but to reach this goal we must acknowledge that God is creating this world ...... **only for the** *righteous.* As kind as we are, as good as we are, and as smart as we are will not be enough. God **must** follow the rule of righteousness so that **Satan can never accuse Him of manipulating the end result of the battle between good and evil**.....and.... for our soul.

Sadly, many do not know that we are *not* granted the forgiveness of our sins if we do not have true remorse for our sins.....those we recognize *and* those we don't. **Not knowing this "rule" for having our sins forgiven cause many to take this sacrament unworthily.... and sadly, many are not aware of this pre-**

requisite. This is because of a *"lack of knowledge"* regarding the sacrament of Holy Communion.

In a world of opposites, when God decided to ban *all* unrighteousness, *all* evil, *all* hate from the new world He is creating; (including Satan and the third of the angels who joined his rebellion), it means that **any unrighteousness we may carry will not and cannot enter that new world.** This includes the sins we commit and also the inherited sin which all men carry as a result of Adam and Eve's fall from grace. It is not that God does not want *all* men to be saved, or that He will not forgive our sins, but that we *cannot* bask in complacency about what is required. We must learn God's words and we *must* watch for where we fall short and make corrections. We must internalize the fact that despite God's longsuffering and forbearance, His gentle heart and His desire that we all understand and accept this incredible plan, He is **bound** by the rule of righteousness. This requires us to learn of and then exercise what this demands of us.

The five virgins who were left behind did not **know** (lack of knowledge) that they would be left behind. They **believed** that they were ready to go. They **wanted** to go and were waiting to go...and they had lived their *life* to go. Yet because of the *absolute* of the rules under which God has chosen to operate in banning evil for all eternity, God was **required** to leave the five foolish virgins behind. It was too late for them to obtain what they **then** recognized they needed.

If we do not want to be left behind, we must ask God to help us recognize where we fall short, what we need to do to be forgiven and make changes before it is too late. We need to know **how** to become all that God longs for us to be. But we will never obtain this understanding if we do not know what is at stake and what God's Plan of Salvation requires. This only comes from knowing what God tells us and scripture provides this.

Sadly, many are conceited and filled with the grandeur of their rhetorical abilities and consider themselves to know what God will and will not accept. They consider their own thought process to be self-sufficient. They are too complacent, too arrogant, and too incredulous about having such restrictions placed on them to consider that we are less than perfect or that God Himself could be **required** under His rule of righteousness to leave us behind to establish a world with no sin or evil for those willing to learn and follow.

Thus to re-cap, each of us should consider what the rules of God's righteousness might mean to them. It may not simply be our heart's attitude or that we participate in the sacrament of Holy Communion which will allow us to be a part of the First Resurrection, it may be the knowledge we still need to acquire to make us worthy of those gifts. We must seriously consider the rules of righteousness under which God has chosen to labor for the good of the new world He will create. We must take care not, as Hosea 4:6 warns, to fall short for "lack of knowledge". *We need to understand what God's righteousness may demand of us* and look into our lives to find those things which we, in our conceit try to justify but which may cause us to become one of the five foolish virgins. **Or....we may choose *not* to do this and suffer the consequences.**

It is the free will... which God gave to each of us.... that we will eventually exercise. God will bring to all who were ever conceived, born or died the same opportunity to learn of Him and become a part of His new kingdom....but not everyone will accept. This then is one of the reasons we must seek to learn and to develop our faith in what we have learned.

"For my people is foolish,
they have not known
me...... they have none
understanding: they are
wise to do evil, but to do
good they have no
knowledge."
Jeremiah 4:22

Chapter Two

THE LACK OF KNOWLEDGE

As mentioned previously, Hosea 4:6, tells us that we may be barred from God's new kingdom because we do not fully understand what is at stake and what is required of us. Hosea 4:6 states: *"My people are destroyed for lack of knowledge, **because thou has rejected knowledge, I will also reject thee** that thou shalt be no priest to me, seeing that thou hast forgotten the law of thy God, I will also forget my children."* This tells us that God realizes that many are not aware of His Plan of Salvation and therefore they are not applying His admonitions to every decision and every choice which is made throughout their daily lives. It tells us that we cannot be a part of the work of God if we do not have an understanding of how we are to discern the spirits, how we are to accept or reject what we see and hear, how we decide what actions to take, and what we accept as truth. God is telling us that *He will hold us responsible for learning* His words.

It can be disconcerting to one new in faith to think that everything in our lives must be based on what pleases our Heavenly Father and what supports His work and His plan for us. It is difficult to think that *everything* from how we interact with our families, how we interact with strangers, how we make our daily decisions, and how we learn right from wrong must be based on what we learn in scripture. Even though we are aware that we seldom exercise the self-control and determination to become the person God wants us to be, we rarely consider that it is through grace that our sins can be forgiven and that we must come to God to obtain that grace. It is through grace that we can also change our nature and develop into the person God wants us to become.

Sadly, we give in to our time constraints, our stress, our exhaustion, and to challenges which distract us from the more important issue of our soul salvation. These provide us with the excuse (justification) to ignore what scripture advises. Luke 6:44 tells us: *"Each tree is recognized by its own fruit."* And Galatians 5:22-23 tells us: *"But the fruit of the spirit is love, joy, peace, kindness, goodness and self-control".* Galatians 5:19-21 warns: *"The acts of a sinful nature are obvious: sexual immorality, impurity, debauchery, idolatry and witchcraft, hatred, discord, jealousy, fits of rage, selfish ambition, dissentions, factions and envy, drunkenness, orgies and the like. I warn you, as I did before, that those like this will not inherit the kingdom of God".* **These are** *but a few* **of the verses in scripture which teach us what we are to do and what we are to avoid.**

When Satan came to Adam and Eve in the Garden of Eden they had no idea that he was evil incarnate; they were influenced by his beauty and his softly spoken words. They were amazed by how he made them think differently than they had before he spoke to them. He beguiled them into doing what God had clearly said they should not do. Yet despite what we know about the fall of Adam and Eve, few seek to learn about the other warnings scripture provides; few desire to learn more about Satan and about why he works against us and against God's plan for our future.

Yet it is because of Satan's influence that few of us compare what we hear in this world to the fruits of the Spirit, and few of us watch for beguiling words from people who subtly negate the principles upon which God wants His children to build their future. Few consider or even understand that Satan is a powerful entity who works in their lives every day, or that scripture clearly tells us that Satan lies to us, can beguile us, can use men to harm us, tempts us, rewards evil, and works day and night to prevent God's Plan of Salvation from coming to fruition. *When we ignore the power and consequences of these facts we are gambling with our eternal life.*

What then would it cost us simply to investigate God's plan and open ourselves to godly wisdom, to knowledge, to how we should examine situations which could impact our eternal future? It is a better gamble to ask God to remove the veil from our eyes and open our understanding to His truths; to what He wants for our lives so that we can learn what is required to develop spiritually. Then **we can make an *informed* decision about where we want to be and what we want to do with this information.** Then we can decide **with knowledge** whether or not to give to God what He requires of those who will be a part of His new kingdom. To do this, we must pray that our Heavenly Father will help us learn what He asks of us and why He asks it, and recognize the subtle traps of evil by discerning those spirits which seek to harm us.

Sadly, many fall prey to fancy rhetoric, especially their own! They fall prey to the promise of an easier, better life, to complacency, to the lies of false doctrines and even to the temptation that we can attend to our spiritual life...later....*after* we reach the temporal goals in which we are engaged. *We also fall prey to the arrogance of thinking we already "know" better and that what scripture tells us is not really necessary to act upon.* We make our dtermination with only a small amount of information. However, scripture tells us that time is running out and that soon grace will be removed and the devastation of the end times will begin.

God has given us the scriptures so we can learn; so we can recognize the ploys which Satan uses to trap us; so we can seriously compare satanic rhetoric to the fruits of the Holy Spirit. Scripture teaches us the signs which God will send to earth to portend the end of grace as we know it. These signs include the worldwide persecution of Christians; children rebelling against authority and hating their parents; sin increasing without remorse; right will be considered wrong and wrong will be considered right; earthquakes, floods, fire, pestilence, famine, and other natural disasters will increase, even in diverse places; men will lie with men; the redistribution of wealth will take place; fear will increase in men's hearts; and an ungodly world leader will arise. Therefore we must ask ourselves if what **we** endorse is godly; if what **we** support is pleasing to God and beneficial to our soul salvation.

Satan is never blatant. He is subtle and clever, and usually unobtrusive...*he does not want to be discovered*...and he laughs when we fall prey to his ploys. He knows that when we believe his lies, he will gain a little more time to wreak havoc on the children of God and a little more time to remain free from the Lake of Fire where he will be bound when God's Plan of Salvation is complete. However, God's Plan of Salvation **will** move forward and **will not** be hampered by what Satan does. Only **we** will be affected by this evil as our faith is tested and our spiritual growth is either enhanced or diminished.

Therefore we must watch, and must seek the knowledge we need to recognize how Satan works, and where and through whom Satan works, and...... what choices we must make to become and remain a faithful child of God. We must be careful not to judge while recognizing and rebuking evil. We must be careful not to lead others to a path which God clearly warns against, but become a role model through which others can find their own soul salvation. And....we must not mock God, or His Plan of Salvation, or the role models and ministers who bring His word to us. Scripture tells us that this angers God and that one day there will be a price to pay for this activity. Scripture forecasts that Christianity itself will be attacked as the time for Christ's return approaches.

As of this writing in most countries in the Middle East, Christians are being attacked; and in Europe fewer and fewer attend church; and in our own country our law-makers work to prevent God's words and the symbols of our faith from being used on public property. This is all in fulfillment of Biblical prophecy. Thus we are being warned to come to God **now;** to listen, to learn, and to *decide with our own free will* after hearing, whether or not to turn to God.

Sadly, many never consider whether learning about God and His plan for our future may be worth the time and effort. They seldom consider that they may change their mind about their temporal goals is they increased their knowledge about God's plan for mankind. To the faithful, to ignore God's incredible offer is beyond comprehension when so much is at stake, especially when one learns what will happen to those who are rejected by God. **God wants to share His kingdom with all of mankind and makes every effort to bring His offer to everyone who ever lived or died.** But the bottom line is that those who love God and thus follow Him, will be those who will be found worthy. We cannot nurture a love for God's Plan of Salavtion with what we do not know.

1 John 3:9-14 gives us this beautiful promise: *"The Lord is not slack concerning his promise, as some men count slackness; but is longsuffering to us-ward, not willing that any should perish, but that all should come to repentance. But **the day of the Lord will come as a thief in the night;** in which the heavens shall pass away with a great noise, and the elements shall melt with fervent heat, the earth also and the works that are therein shall be burned up. Seeing then that all these things shall be dissolved, **what manner of persons ought ye to be** in all holy conversation and godliness. Looking for and hasting unto the coming of the day of God, wherein the heavens being on fire shall be dissolved, and the elements shall melt with fervent heat? Nevertheless we, according to his promise, look for new heavens and a new earth, wherein dwelleth righteousness. Wherefore, beloved, **seeing that**

ye look for such things, be diligent that ye may be found of him in peace, without spot, blameless. "

God has promised that every man, woman and child will hear His offer; learn what He wants to give them if they will just trust and follow Him. God's words; such as are quoted in this book, will be brought to everyone at one time or another. Thus no one will ever be able to say that they were not told. They will know how and when they accepted or rejected what God was offering them. That day will be Judgment Day when all we did or did not do will be weighed. It will be a joyous experience for many and a very sad and devastating experience for others.

Faith in God's Plan of Salvation cannot be sustained when one does not know this plan or why it was conceived or what it's goal is. Faith cannot grow in a vacuum of ignorance regarding what scripture tells us.

> "Let the wicked forsake his way, and the unrighteous man his thoughts; and let him return unto the Lord......."
>
> Isaiah 55:7

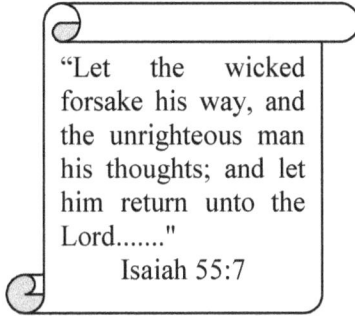

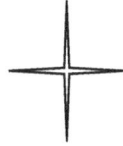

Chapter Three

THE FIRST AND LAST LIE

Spiritual warfare is a phrase which we rarely hear, let alone discuss. Yet without our knowledge, every day of our lives, every man, woman, and child is subjected to the battle between good and evil; between God and Satan for their soul. Satan himself, who is the leader of the fallen angels, directs his followers to separate us from God. Satan's desire is to block our awareness that evil is real and active in our lives and that Satan works to place indifference, confusion, complacency or arrogant self doctrines into our hearts to prevent us from learning about and accepting God's Plan of Salvation for mankind.

Most of us struggle with our faith because **we have succumbed to the satanic lie that because God is such a loving God, he automatically *and without much work on our part,* forgives us and will accept us, just as we are.** Satan has been very successful in causing many to accept this theory as fact and become unconcerned about the future of their soul. The subtlety of this lie, which originated with Satan, is found in the story of the Creation. As we read about the relationship which Adam and Eve had with God, we learn that God asked only that they respect and honor His request *not* to eat the fruit from **one** of the many trees in the Garden of Eden. As they walked in the garden God created for them, and they freely conversed with God they were happy. And from that happiness scripture gives us one of the most interesting verses in the Bible. This verse is found in Genesis 2:25 and reads, *"And they were both naked, the man and his wife, and **were not ashamed.**"* Thus, at that point in time both Adam and Eve had absolutely nothing to hide.... from God or from one another. They were free of sin, free of deceit, free of guile, free of anything which could cause them to be embarrassed or ashamed....or worried. They carried no guilt, felt no pain, endured no suffering, and had no dishonor in them. But following this verse, we are immediately introduced to the incredible subtly of the serpent who wanted to take this happiness away from them. The very first words in this verse tell us: *"Now the serpent was more subtle than any beast........"* (Genesis 3:1)

If we examine what Webster's Dictionary tells us about the word "subtle" we learn that it is "the ability to penetrate deeply and thoroughly". It also means **"cunningly contrived",** "highly skillful "and "operating insidiously". Armed with this definition and reading further in that verse in Genesis, we see that the serpent then posed a question: *"Ye shall **not** eat of **every** tree in the garden?"* If we take a close look at those words we can understand why **they became the first lie**; the first lying innuendo known to man. Those words implied, simply by asking a question, that Eve must have misunderstood God's instructions; that *surely* God could **not** have meant that they should be deprived of such a benefit. The words implied that *surely* God had made the **entire** Garden of Eden for them so why would He deny them such a small part of it? This certainly piqued the curiosity of Adam and Eve and made them trust their own...and new...understanding of God's words. This first lie took root in the heart of man.

In many parts of scripture we are taught that God never changes; that He is the same today as He was yesterday; that His laws and statutes do not change; that only grace has brought the change **mankind** required so they could again become a part of the community of God. And one of the true and beautiful miracles of scripture is that God will always open our understanding when we ask Him and seek to learn. Thus when we study how God wove the beginning of His Plan of Salvation right into the culmination of that plan, we learn how incredibly accurate and perfect scripture is.

When we move ahead to examine the *last* lie in Biblical history we can see how very similar it is to the first lie. While the first lie affected not only one couple but everyone born thereafter through inherited sin, the last lie touches everyone in the world as well. What we learn from this is that Satan's tactics to separate man from God has never changed either, but that man's fallibility...*when he does not know God's words*......has greatly increased.

The last lie and the one which will cause many to fall away from their faith and lose their soul salvation is today's application of political correctness. This last lie is fathered by the same deceiver who fathered the first lie....the serpent, Satan. Political correctness is a satanic scourge which puts forth to all of mankind the same question which was put to Eve. What it *really* suggests through posing yet another question is: "You *can't* have it both ways?....*why*?" Satan frames his question as a challenge to man and his subtle words imply: "Ye shall *not* bend God's words so you can become a more loving and compassionate person?"

What this makes man believe is that he *must* bend God's words to show that God *is* forgiving and loving and compassionate and therefore *we* must become the compassionate, forgiving, understanding soul God wants by *also* bending those rules. *And thus is born the entrapment of good people all over the world* through their ego and desire to *appear* to be "good" people. Sadly, this false goodness is in the eyes of the world and not in the eyes of God. It is the *lack of understanding* and lack of trust in God's statutes which has allowed this lie to become so believable. This lie has spawned dishonesty and dishonor by implying that it serves the greater good. However it is simply deceit; it is a justification which implies **that we must allow sin so**

we do not anger anyone with the truth and we do not judge. It has spawned sinful behavior with the assumption that one cannot change; cannot and should not be required to change. It has desecrated the sacrament of Holy Communion by allowing it to be taken unworthily by condoning sin **under the guise of not judging**.

Sadly many of these politically correct arguments appear kind and compassionate and cause confusion in the children of God. We no longer recognize right from wrong and no longer have the backbone to stand up for what God tells us in scripture. *In the politically correct quest to show compassion and not judge, sin and ungodly behavior is excused, even condoned and supported.* It is justified by the Adam-like nature of those who commit those sins **and those who allow them by condoning them**.

Sadly, this is an artificial "goodness" which is created around those who excuse ungodly behavior. This "doctrine" fills churches with those who want **no constraints** on their actions or interactions or on what Holy Communion actually requires. **It negates what taking Holy Communion worthily does demand of every individual**. Further, political correctness has determined that the "rules" laid down by scripture are "old fashioned" and that scripture is "**not fit for the times in which we live**". This occurs despite the fact that God and His statutes are the same today as they were yesterday and that not one word of scripture is to be changed. (Revelation 22:19)

In the fourth verse of Genesis 3, as we read about that first lie, we read that the serpent said to Eve: *"Ye shall **not** surely die"*. Here we can see that this lie, offered so long ago by the serpent is the same lie Satan perpetuates today. If Satan blatantly said instead: "Go and sin with abandon and *still* ye shall not die as God says because He forgives everything anyway", perhaps we would think twice about our actions. In verse 5 of Genesis 3 we read: *"For God doth know....your eyes shall be opened, and **ye shall be as gods, knowing** good and evil."*

Amazingly, this is exactly what political correctness tells us. That now, having "matured" as a country and a people, *we finally understand compassion and forgiveness and thereby do act "as Gods"*. Therefore what is **now** preached through political correctness is that God wants us to look the other way in the face of sin, do whatever makes us happy, or whatever we can justify, and never rebuke, chastise or teach what scripture tells us regarding sin. It also supports the idea that all sin is forgiven **even when we have no remorse for those sins.**

The truth however, is that to have our sins forgiven we **must** *acknowledge* that what we did *was* a sin in the eyes of God; we must **have** *remorse* for having committed that sin; and we must honestly wish, hope and work toward *not committing that sin again...even if we fail over and over*. We also have to *forgive* those who may have brought us harm or mocked us for believing and upholding God's words. The truth is that God's admonitions .... *and not man's determinations*..... teach what sin is.....both yesterday and today, and that while God *will* forgive our sin, *certain conditions exist for us to obtain forgiveness.*

In Genesis 3:8 we read that because of their disobedience, Adam and Eve then hid from the Lord. This marks the first human form of deceit. What they did dishonored God and their relationship with Him; it spawned the first "blame game" where Adam blamed his sin and deceit on Eve; it caused the first enmity to emerge between two people when they lied, and it created the patterns by which all of mankind could become trapped in sin.

God does not require that we reach perfection here on earth, but does require that we are free of sin when we enter eternity. This gift is provided only through the sacrifice of Christ and thus the *worthy* application of Holy Communion **with all its rules and regulations and pre-requisites.** If there is *any* action we take which we try to hide, we must understand that it is deceit and it is dishonorable. Yet today's world operates on a "what they don't know won't hurt them" concept and welcomes deceit as a form of protecting our selfish personal goals by *pretending* to care about the feelings of others when we care only for ourselves. Real love is tough love and it admonishes to prevent damage to our soul and to our relationship with God. False love smoothes sin over and looks the other way telling us: *"surely God didn't mean...."*

Compromise is another word which may describe these attitudes. Compromise supports the Adam-like nature which **wants *what it wants* regardless of how it gets it.** Adding to this confusion is the world's desire for power and the fear many parents have about rejection. By allowing everyone to do as they please.... votes are gained..... the parent/child conflict is lessened..... common ground is established between governments..... different religions meld through false doctrines..... and God's words fall on deaf ears. Confusion spawns complacency. Complacency destroys the order which God wants for mankind for the benefit of their soul salvation... and harms our quest for a world free of sin.

Many have wondered why the number God longs for to fill the role as the Bride of Christ is indicated in scripture as an incredibly low figure. Many have ascribed that number to an allegorical figure. But as we see churches, and children of God slipping into accepting the last lie through political correctness, it is easier to understand why God tells us that this number will be so small. Nevertheless, **God,** in His righteousness **will find those souls who will *not* sell out and *will* stand firm for His statutes.**

Parents must ask themselves what price they will pay if they accept this last lie. They must understand that the highest price will be paid by their children as they grow up in a world without restrictions on sin; in a world which encourages sin and discourages the loyalties expected from the family of God. This will cause both parents and children to lose their soul salvation and will be **a result of the failure of the parents to teach their children about God.** Sadly, families no longer discipline their children and parents and schools no longer teach Biblical values, but do teach the lie of political correctness. The price for this is also noted in the increase of enmity between people throughout the entire world even among the children of God. It affects the number of souls who will found worthy when Christ returns.

While 144,000 might be a symbolic number which scripture provides to define who will be a part of the Bride of Christ, *comparatively and percentage-wise, this number clearly warns us that few souls will meet the criteria God has set for His Holy Family.* Yes, there will still be the lambs for Heaven, but do we want to begin and end our life of faith not understanding what changes we need to make to be one of those 144,000, symbolic figure or not? This choice faces us today; now. We must ask what we want for our future and **the future of those we love**. What are we willing to do to obtain that future? To which standards we will hold fast? And are we are willing to place Biblical values into our hearts and fight for them *even when we are labeled a holy-roller or a religious fanatic?*

It is all about our free will and how we exercise it. And during these end times there is a greater intensity on Satan's part to push us into using our free will for religious debate rather than serious learning. Sadly, for today's generation it is a **lack of knowledge** coupled with the incredibly powerful influence of the great *last* lie which justifies disloyalty, dishonor and all types of sin. **There is little time**, and little incentive to stand up and be counted for God because in these end times those who do will be mocked and their testimony will be ridiculed. Christianity itself will be persecuted and many will become so indoctrinated by that last lie that they can no longer see the truth in God's words and....may never even hear them.

However, for those who do stand firm in their faith, God promises to provide help. God does watch over us and hears our prayers. God teaches us through scripture that knowing His words is like wearing protective armour, and that the forgiveness of sin keeps us free of the enslavement which hands us over to Satan. The angels who remain faithful to God help mankind battle these satanic spirits. They use their powers to guide us toward recognizing what *is* truth. They help us discern the evil spirits, to better understand God's offer, to desire to be a part of God's future, to seek the forgiveness of sin, and to strive to become all God wants us to become.....but only if we ask for it and try to live by what God tells us. They help us increase our faith.

Just as it takes abstinence to lose weight or stop smoking or to overcome many of the habits we have developed which can be harmful to us, so too it takes a desire for abstinence from sin to become a part of the Bride of Christ. A true "desire" not to sin does not mean that we do not fail from time to time. It means that we have remorse when we do and that we truly love God so much that we want to overcome our sinful tendencies. God clearly tells us what is a sin, and He clearly tells us that we are all sinners. Therefore He fully understands that because of our Adam-like nature and the strength of Satan and His fallen angels, we cannot be sin-free.

Thus, we must turn to God for grace and for help to do better each day. God's help is the strongest help we can ask for. When we understand God's words and we understand the power of Satan we realize that we need God. Because of Adam and Eve's sin and thus the Adam-like and sinful nature with which we were born, John 8:44-45 warns: *"Ye are of your father the devil, and the lusts of your father ye will do........because there was no truth in him. When he speaketh a lie; he speaketh of his own: for he is a liar, and the father of it. And because I tell you the truth, ye believe me not."* But as we change and desire to shed that nature, and therefore strive to do so, God promises us an incredible future and...He increases our faith in it!

Proverbs 3:5-10 tells us: *"Trust in the LORD with all thine heart; and lean not toward thine own understanding. In all they ways acknowledge him, and he shall deliver thy paths. Be not wise in thine own eyes: fear the LORD and depart from evil. It shall be health to thy navel, and marrow to thy bones. Honour the LORD with thy substance and with the firstfruits of all thy increase: so shall thy barns be filled with plenty and thy presses shall burst out with new wine."*

These verses give us a great deal of information. First of all they tell us that God will look after us and will make sure that we always have what we need if we are seeking Him and striving to do His will. But they also tell us to **beware of our own thoughts and to fear God enough to learn His ways and make His ways *become* our thoughts.** Scripture teaches us to acknowledge God in all things, to honour Him, and to depart from evil. Then, to seek His word, to thank Him, to tithe and to remember that all that we have comes from God. To demonstrate our thankfulness for what God has provided, we are to return a part what He has given us, in the form of a tithe. When we do this, we are told in those verses that we will never want for anything we need.

God's words are filled with beautiful promises and twice warns us to trust what God tells us rather than try to make sense out of what the world tells us, or become so arrogant in our own wisdom that we begin to believe that our opinions are better than God's. As we begin to understand God's plan and understand God's advice and the promises He provides, we come to a crossroad where we either accept or reject what we have learned. God warns us not to be lukewarm, but to make the commitment to Him **with all our heart**.......or not. Revelation 3:16 warns: *"So, because you are lukewarm, and neither hot nor cold, I will spit you out of my mouth."*

In other words, God wants our love and a commitment to that love and to His way of life so that a people of one goal, one mind, and one heart can live in harmony and joy for all eternity. And God will bless us when we embark on this path to learn of Him and commit ourselves to doing His will as best we can. And....He will forgive us when we fail... if we have remorse for those failures. He will also bless us for every effort we make.

1 Corinthians 17:26-27 says: *"And now Lord, Thou art God, And hast promised this goodness unto Thy servant. Now therefore let*

it please Thee to bless the house of Thy servant, that it may before Thee forever; For Thou blesses O Lord, and it shall be blessed forever." In return, God only asks that we love Him and those He loves. While these words seem easy on the surface, what they really mean is that if we profess our love for our Heavenly Father, we must make our deeds match our words, To love someone requires loyalty, trust and a close relationship. These then are what we must take on as our responsibility: to desire, to seek, to build a loving and intimate relationship with God. These actions guarantee that our faith will increase.

"And I will utter my judgments against them touching all their wickedness, who have forsaken me.... and worshipped the works of their own hands."
Jeremiah 1:16

Chapter Four

THE REBELLING BODY

As we near the day when Christ will return, Satan's anger and desperation will increase and he will vehemently attack the children of God using deadly force. He will cause many to doubt that God exists. He will do this by causing a myriad of fears; perhaps through a sense of loneliness, through contention, or financial burden, some may face a grave illness, and others will be led into absolute complacency in matters pertaining to God. He will cause many to sin, many to be confused, and even the faithful to question why God does not step into to right the many wrongs in this world. He will cause great multitudes to be so "politically correct" about all things that they are no longer concerned about God's statutes. Whichever way Satan attacks to bring suffering to the children of God, it will almost surely also cause the debilitating effects of emotional pain. Satan will work in this manner until our hearts and minds are filled with worry and fear. God knows this and he provides a means of escape for us. God tells us to help one another; to support one another when we go through these attacks.

Scripture tells is that to help counter these satanic attacks, the children of God who desire to remain faithful need to reach out to one another to help ease whatever burdens we face. We must strengthen one another. We can find solace with other believers because they too have been or are under satanic attack and understand what we are going through and why. If someone has already experienced a situation or a period of time which was very difficult to bear; perhaps very similar to what we are going through; they will have the empathy and wisdom to help us.

This is why a child of God must help **identify the miracle of faith which our various burdens have produced in the past.** We must teach others how to avoid focusing on how our body is reacting to our current concerns. We may commiserate about how bad we feel, how fearful we are, what disappointments we have experienced, how angry we may be, and why God allowed those circumstances into our lives. But in the end, if we **recall the blessing God has always brought out of all these burdens,** this will increase our faith and decrease our anxiety.

As we read the book of Job in the Bible we learn that God considered Job to be *"perfect and upright, and one that feared God, and eschewed evil"*. (Job 1:1, 8) Despite these attributes, God allowed Satan to take Job's entire material life away from him: his wife, his children, his home, his money, his servants, his animals, and even his friends. Job felt all of the painful emotions we feel and certainly an even greater sadness. But Satan was warned by God not to kill him. (Job 1:12)

Because of Job's faith in God which Satan was trying desperately to break, Job's reaction to his burdens was to say, *"...Naked came I out of my mother's womb, and naked I shall return thither; the Lord gave, and **the Lord hath taken away.; blessed be the name of the Lord."*** (Job 1:21) Thus we know that amazingly Job never blamed God for his misfortune. Satan was furious when Job could not be broken by what was taken from him. Satan was not satisfied with the harm he'd already brought Job and therefore went back to God again asking Him if he could bring harm to Job's body. Satan felt that this would finally break Job and prove that Job would then forsake God. (Job 2:3) God gave this permission to Satan but again warned him not to kill him.

Satan then smote Job with boils from the sole of his foot to his head. (Job 2:7) Job still remained in love with and faithful to his Heavenly Father asking "...*shall we receive good at the hand of God, and shall we not receive evil.*" (Job 2:10) Nevertheless Job's grief, according to scripture, was "*very great*". (Job 2:13) In fact, at this point Job was in so much pain emotionally *and* physically that he wondered why he'd been born, why he didn't die while still in the womb. He understood why some longed for death and wondered why they could not find it. He admitted that *all that he feared in life had come upon him.* (Job 3:25)

But as Job spoke, he began to understand his dependence upon God and how fragile his personal control really was. He told God that he would commit his cause to Him (Job 5:8) and understood and accepted what was happening. He said "*....happy is the man whom God correcteth; therefore despise not thou the chastening of the Almighty.*" (Job 5:17)

This story of Job shows us that Job gained a new realization of his everlasting attachment to God no matter what circumstances he had to endure. It was an awakening in his heart and soul of his commitment. It was also a new awareness of the trust that **no matter what happened, his love for God would not waver** and God would bring him through his circumstances. God already knew that this reaction lived in Job's heart.....but Job had not known this. It was this experience which gave Job a greater trust and understanding of his own personal commitment to God. (Job 5:20-27)

Nevertheless, Job suffered. A sense of grief, of calamity, of terror and sorrow came at him. (Job 6:1-10) Despite a wish to die to ease his pain, his inner strength and trust remained. (Job 6:10-

13) Then Job asked God to **teach him, to "cause" him to understand despite his desperate words**. (Job 6:24-26) In fact, Job also admits to having lost his hope. (Job 7:6) In Chapter 9 Job we again see Job's commitment to God not wavering as he talks about the greatness of God and how insignificant man is in comparison. He understands that man is unable to justify himself before the perfection of God.

Through this conversation, **Job glorified God** and **humbled himself,** admitting to a confusion about what God asked of him. (Job 10:15) And in Chapter 13, Job tells his friend how much he would like to reason with God but understands how God's majesty and man's deceitfulness could hinder that process. Then Job simply turns his life over to God despite his pain and says, "...*all the days of my appointed time* **will I wait**, *till my change come.*" (Job 14:14) Job also admits that though he speaks of it, his pain is not eased (Job 16:6) and that he knows that God has **allowed Satan** to "***break him,*** *take him by his neck, shake him*", (Job 16:12) and admits that his face is "*foul with weeping*" (Job 16:16)

What we can learn from this is that as **we** suffer and as our bodies rebel from the pain we are enduring, we are recognizing our commitment to God and proving to ourselves that with God we can endure all things. We learn that we can speak *against* those occurrences and we can hate our circumstance and our pain, **but will still remain faithful and continue to trust God with our lives.** Whether or not we have lost our family, our friends, or are forgotten by our kinfolk (Job 19:13-20), we can trust that God is with us. We will have proven our trust in God as Job did when he said "*For I know that my redeemer liveth, and that he shall stand at the latter day upon the earth........whom I shall see myself, and my eyes shall behold....*" (Job 19:25-27)

At one point Job even wondered what he should do about his circumstances and says: "*Behold, I go forward, but* ***he is not there****; and backward, but* ***I cannot perceive him.***" (Job 23:8) yet Job follows up by *saying "But* ***he knoweth the way that I take***:

*when he hath tried me **I shall come forth as gold**."* (Job 23:10) Then Job explains, *"...where is the place of understanding? Man knoweth not the price therof......it cannot be gotten for gold..... sapphire..... coral... pearls....."* (Job 28:12-20) and then says, *"...Behold, the fear of the Lord; **that is wisdom**; and to depart from evil is understanding."* (Job 28:28) And then God spoke directly to Job describing His power (Job 40:6-24, Job 41:1-34) and finally God **released Job from Satan's captivity** and blessed him with double what he had before. (Job 42:10) Job lived to be 140 years old and did so with God's blessing...**<u>not because he hadn't complained or asked questions, but because he remained faithful and acknowledged God's right to do with him as He deemed necessary.</u>**

Therefore, whatever we suffer, however our bodies rebel against our circumstances it is our hearts attitude, our submission, our understanding and our love for God which will matter. We needn't feel guilty to wonder why we suffer, or worry when we ask God to release us from our pain. We need only to accept God as the master of our lives and trust Him to bring us through our circumstances once we have learned the lesson it is to bring us. We need to trust that God **always** creates something special from the ashes of our sorrow. We need to be **willing** to learn and to follow God's will and then trust that *we will emerge a better person for having endured that experience* and a more suitable bride His Son. We need to build the faith we will require when we are tested. We need to love God with all our heart and love those who God loves and.....**know God's words** so we can follow them.

Sadly, many "believe" without having the kind of faith that can be tested. They "believe" in God, "believe" that Christ is the Son of God and "believe" that Christ died for us to provide a pathway for the forgiveness of our sins. But faith, *true faith* means that we believe so strongly that we trust God's decisions for our lives completely, **and that we trust what God tells us** through scripture. **This includes the "rules" or statutes God lays out for us, and thus our compliance with them.** We willingly endure our lessons, strive to learn from them, so that we can reach the goal of our faith.

Scripture tells us that there are pre-requisites for the forgiveness of sin, and thereby tells us what God considers a sin. Because we "believe", because we "trust", we try to follow. When we can finally submit to God's will even though we complain and worry and wish our life could be different, we can rest assured that our faith has increased and we have touched God's heart through our submission. This is how we can subdue the Adam-like nature which God has asked us to shed and begun the process of becoming more Christ-like. We are on the road to becoming all that God sees in us!

Hebrews 11:6 tells us: But without faith, it is impossible to please Him: for he that cometh to God must believe that He is...."

> "Then opened he their understanding that they might understand the scriptures."
>
> Luke 24:45

Chapter Five

SATAN AND THE FALLEN ANGELS

Scripture tells us that before Satan waged war against God he was called Lucifer and was the most beautiful angel in heaven. He waged his war because of his jealousy of Christ and the jealously that ate at him when he learned that God planned to elevate the new creation of mankind to a position higher than the angels. Because his beauty and power was so immense, Lucifer was able to draw one third of all the angels in heaven to his cause. His goal was to thwart God's Plan of Salvation and become the ruler of heaven. As a result of his actions, he and his fallen angels were no longer allowed to live in Heaven.

Some Biblical scholars believe that Lucifer had been the chief of all angels and was assigned to the angelic rank called the *Powers*. Most believe that it is he who is referenced by the words *"ruler"* and *"prince"* of the darkness of this world, and that he and his fallen angels are what the Bible calls *"spiritual wickedness in high places"*. Ephesians 2:2 speaks of Satan's past and present with the words: *"Wherein in time past ye walked according to the **prince of the power**, the spirit that now worketh in the children of disobedience."*

Satan has many names. He was, of course originally known as Lucifer. When he lost his position in heaven he was called the Devil, Satan, Beelzebub, the Prince of darkness, the serpent, the father of lies, and many other names. Luke 11:15 tells us that Beelzebub (Satan) is the chief of devils and has authority over all the demons who work on his behalf to break the faith of God's children. When Satan and his followers waged war against God, they were overcome and were thrown out of heaven to the earth. Thus, Satan and the angels who joined his rebellion became the demons who work to prevent man from learning of and obeying God. They realize that if man disobeys God just as they did, man cannot reside with God. They also believe that under these circumstances God's Plan of Salvation cannot be completed. They believe that delaying the completion of God's Plan of Salvation will allow them to retain their power in the earthly kingdom over which they (Satan and the fallen angels) currently reign. This, they believe, will allow them to escape punishment even if only temporarily, for their rebellion. They are to be bound with all evil in the Lake of Fire for all eternity.

Satan used his powers to tempt Adam and Eve to sin. From that day forward, the fallen angels who followed Satan and retained the powers of their rank, began to use that power against all of mankind hoping to prevent God's Plan of Salvation from being completed. Nevertheless, God's plan does move forward and *will* be completed and *every* fallen angel who harmed God's children and rebelled against God will be thrown into the Lake of Fire with Satan. With them will be those people, the unredeemed, who chose, of their own free will, not to follow God's statutes. Thus Satan, his angels, and the unredeemed souls of mankind will be placed into the Lake of Fire, also known as Hell, and remain there for all eternity forever separated from God. They will be *continuously* tormented by hatred, anger, envy, jealousy, back biting, cruelty, lies, slander and all things evil. It is through God's Plan of Salvation that good and evil will be separated and evil will not be allowed to enter God's new kingdom and will instead be bound forever in hell....in the Lake of Fire.

To thwart Satan's plan to prevent God from touching the hearts of all mankind to draw them away from sin, God gave man prophets like Samuel, Moses and others, and also gave them the Old Testament of the Bible. Then when Christ brought mankind His sacrifice which offered man redemption from sin, God developed Apostles and ministers to bring His people the knowledge they required to understand the grace they were being offered. God also gave mankind the New Testament of the Bible through which all people could learn even more. Through the Holy Spirit of God, these Apostles and Ministers, and these writings would bring mankind the wisdom they would need to understand Satan and the fallen angels, and learn of the sacrifice Christ made to pay the ransom demanded by sin.

Scripture explains that these powerful fallen angels bring sin to mankind not only because of the evil in their heart, but because of their need to retain their freedom. They attack man with a vengeance, desperately trying to delay the completion of God's plan and thus delay when they will be bound forever. Often **these attacks are so subtle that man is unaware of the damage they do to his soul.** Scripture teaches us how to recognize and fight these attacks and also how to be free of the sin with which Satan and his demons tempt us. Ephesians 6:11-12 tells us: *"Put on the whole armour of God, that ye may be able to **stand against the wiles of the devil.** For **we wrestle not against flesh and blood but against principalities, against powers, against the rulers of the darkness of this world, against spiritual wickedness in high places.**"*

In Luke 11:20-22, we are also told that God is more powerful than Satan and that God has given His Apostles the power to cast these devils out of man. However, Luke 24-26 warns that ***these spirits can come back* and re-enter man** if he does not *truly* repent, and that they can fill our soul with ungodly endeavors, with complacency, and with the false doctrines and opinions which can force the Holy Spirit to leave.

Even Christ makes mention of the powerful position which Satan holds in our world by calling him a prince when speaking about his eventual demise. In John 12:31 Christ tells us: *"Now is the judgment of this world, now shall **the prince of this world** be cast out."* God, out of His perfect love and understanding, knows that Satan and those who follow him work to tempt us to sin, thus God offers to forgive our sins. The pre-requisites for that forgiveness are that we ***acknowledge* our sins, have *remorse* for them, *strive* not to commit those sins again, and that we willingly *forgive* others.** Therefore as Satan works to cause us to sin, he also works to make us forget to acknowledge not only the sins we have *committed knowingly and unknowingly* but also those sins of *omission* which are the actions God asks us to take which we do not take.

Scripture, God's direct instruction and comfort, provides us with every nuance of God's plan for mankind and how Satan works to prevent that plan from being completed. It teaches us to look *inward* so we can spurn those attacks and watch for even those seven deadly sins which are so hard to discern. It teaches us why it is necessary to learn God's words and strive to understand all that He wants to tell us. As God's words unfold and we recognize the qualities required in those God wants for His kingdom, we realize that we have much to learn. We must change. God's statutes teach us that we must **adjust** our thoughts and actions to God's words, **shed** our old nature and our arrogant know-it all nature to **become** more loving, more giving, more understanding, and **take** on the Christ-like nature God longs for.

But ***if we don't know all the little parts which make up the whole, we do not have the tools by which we can grow into that nature, nor know how to recognize the work of Satan and his followers.*** Nor will we understand that Satan's followers can unleash natural disasters, cause unrest in families, inspire evil in our leaders, cause spiritual complacency, and cause man to believe that there is no God who can or will control such activity. The Holy Spirit however, can help us fully understand these mysteries, avoid satanic traps, recognize our sins, and desire forgiveness.

I Peter 3:22 tells us: *"Who is gone into heaven, And is on the right hand of God; angels and authorities and powers being made subject unto him."* This teaches us that Christ holds ultimate power over **all** the angels. 1 Peter 5:8 warns: *"Be sober, be vigilant, because your **adversary the devil**, as a roaring lion, walketh about, seeking who he may devour."* Hebrews 10:14, 17 tells us: *"For by one offering he hath perfected for ever them that are sanctified. And their sins and iniquities will I remember no more."* As these end time prophecies are fulfilled, God warns in Mark 13:20: *"And except that the Lord hath shortened, those days, **no flesh should be saved**; but for the elect's sake, whom he hath chosen, he hath shortened them."*

God wants us to value love, trust, honesty, and loyalty, and to practice these attributes *voluntarily* . He wants us to tap into the power which the sacrifice of Christ affords the children of God. (John 14:23) Colossians 1:13 tells us that the triumph of Christ *"....hath **delivered us from the power of darkness**, and hath translated us into the kingdom of His dear Son."* Christ could have overpowered the evil forces which brought Him before those who crucified Him, but Romans 13:1-7 explains that God allowed those satanic forces to exercise their power not only to bring mankind forgiveness, but also **to fulfill the words of scripture** and execute the prophecies foretelling the sacrifice of Christ.

As we learn, we are strengthened. Our faith is strengthened. We begin to see that God ultimately controls everything. He purposely gave authority to the evil powers so that prophecy would be fulfilled; so that mankind would turn again to God, would trust God and desire to leave all things evil behind. Therefore the fallen angels exercise their powers to produce evil rather than good because **God allows their activity for the development of man's soul.** Man will have to use his free will to decide **who** he will follow.

But once again, this requires that man learn of God, learn His words, learn what His Plan of Salvation is, and then ultimately make the decision himself to believe and strive to follow, or not.

Romans 10:17 tells us: *"So then faith comes by hearing, and hearing by the word of God."* This helps us understand that as we learn (hear) God's words, our faith will increase. This is a promise which God makes to us.

"For God shall bring every work into judgment, with every secret thing, whether it be good, or whether it be evil."
Ecclesiastes 12:14

Chapter Six

GOD'S GARDEN

Scripture opens with a description of how God created our world and began the incredible task of creating the souls with whom He wants to share His kingdom. The Creation was the first step in the process to teach mankind about God; His creativity, His appreciation for beauty and diversity; His giving heart; and what kind of future He wishes to provide for us. As we read more about the Creation, we begin to understand that all He did, He did for us and that everything He created in that time, He saw as good. (Genesis 1:10) As our Heavenly Father continued His magnificent work, He brought into being many grasses, seeds, and fruit trees, which He also saw as good. (Genesis 1:11-12) And when everything God created for our benefit was in place, Genesis 1:31 tells us that He considered it all *"very good"*! This tells us that what God created contained no evil and no sin...it was perfect.

To discern what God seeks to teach us through His creation we must first recognize that what God so lovingly created was incredibly diverse. He designed birds to be magnificently different in shape and size and color, in song and flight. He designed trees of every size; tall and small, thin and wide, some with fruit and some without, some with needles and some with leaves. The leaves were of every shape and size as well and many changed with the seasons. He designed the seas to be calm **and** stormy, and dependent upon the pull of the moon. He designed the skies to hold clouds of every size and shape which are moved slowly or quickly depending upon the changing winds.

When we study what God created and seek to learn from it, we can see that God is not only providing for us materially, but also spiritually. The diversity of His creation teaches us to view not only the differences in birds and animals and flora and fauna as *beautiful and beneficial*, but also to appreciate the differences in mankind as well. These things also teach us about God's incredible power and ability. They teach us about the beauty and ease He wants to provide for us, how He wants us to view the differences in the creation through His eyes and thereby learn from those differences. In Genesis 2:8 we read: *"And the Lord God planted a garden eastward in Eden and there He put the man whom He had formed."* This garden can teach us what God planted and why.

Even in our horticultural ignorance we know that some flowers were created for their immediate beauty so we would be quickly drawn to them. Through these we recognize the artistic quality of what God created and are made ready to acknowledge the beauty and generosity in God's heart. But our Heavenly Father also planted many other flowers in the garden, some not as beautiful, but each to bring us a valuable lesson. Some were created to have great strength to teach us about endurance. Some were created for their exquisite aroma which God likens to our offerings. (Genesis 8:21, Ephesians 5:2) Some flowers were created with dense foliage to demonstrate how they retain their place in the garden and teach us to fill ourselves with God's words so we do not allow evil to rob us of our place in Heaven.

Others spread from their planting with a delicately cascading grace to show us that we too must reach out to others with the offer of God's grace. Some flowers may not offer a surface beauty yet provide great value because God implanted within them the ability to heal through their medicinal components. This teaches us that we can offer healing to others if we have healed our own heart and that sometimes our own value may lie beneath the surface. God's garden clearly demonstrates that though flowers are different, one flower is not "better" than another. Each has a place in God's garden and each can proclaim the gift God gave them when He created them. Though different, though their value is sometimes hidden, *God created them for a purpose and He wants them to fulfill that purpose.*

Thus everything God created was good, everything worked together in harmony, and was equally blessed. But when sin entered the world the blessing was lost and a curse came upon the entire creation. What had once worked in harmony began to fall into disharmony. Instead of appreciating their differences, suddenly, under the curse, one flower grew so tall that it stole the sun from another. One flower grew deeper roots to steal water from its neighbor. One plant began to demand and create an alkaline soil, while another demanded an acid soil. Some became poisonous, hiding their venomous nature under the guise of their beauty. The flowers had fallen under the curse of sin and were transformed. This shows us that **we** must avoid the curse of sin which may poison and transform our soul.

Just as He did with the flowers, God purposely created differences in people to teach us the joy and harmony which can exist in a unique and varied creation. He wants us to appreciate what He created; to learn the value of each difference, and to respect that each has equal value in His eyes and a function; a talent. Thus, while we are different from one another; each has **great** value. We lose that blessing however when we do not do as God asks us to do, and when we do not heed the warnings He provides for us or do not spurn what He tells us is sin. God's children must understand that we are to celebrate our differences as long as they are godly, and learn from them; that we are to fight against and even run from those who, under the curse of evil, offer hate and bring harm.

God wants us to appreciate what we have and what we are, rather than envy those who we foolishly believe are more or better, or denigrate those who we falsely believe are less or inferior. Appreciation for what we have rather than what we want is an important aspect of being content. *Appreciation for others touches God's heart.* Just like the flowers, God has created people with black hair, brown hair, and some with blonde hair. He has created us with brown skin, black skin, white skin, yellow skin, red skin, and almost everything in between. He has created people who are tall and short, stocky and thin, with brown eyes or amber eyes, blue eyes or hazel eyes. Some may smile while others frown. Some need attention and others prefer to stay in the shadows.

But **just as Satan entered God's garden to interject thorns and weeds and poisons to pervert the plants, so has he entered man to pervert them to pride, arrogance, self-satisfaction, envy, hatred, racism, sin, and a sense of superiority or inferiority.** He perverts our thoughts to destroy our understanding that God created and loves the diversity in man just as He created and loves the diversity in nature, **though He hates man's sin.** *Each flower and each person is equal to another through the very uniqueness God granted them and through the acknowledgement and forgiveness of sin.*

God also created our ability to love, to hope, to trust, and **to develop a special talent which He hopes we will nurture and use in His service.** Despite our failures, God wants us to put aside the Adam-like nature which **accepts** sin and turn to the Christ-like nature which fights sin and appreciates a kind and gentle nature. Free will allows us to decide which attitude and which nature we will embrace. *Free will allows us to decide to be thankful and loving and sin-free or to be angry and hateful and sinful. Free will forces us to take responsibility for our choice;, what those choices bring into our lives; and what they will ultimately mean to God and to our soul salvation.*

Scripture teaches us that, through prayer, God helps us recognize what our mistakes have been and to carefully consider the beam in our own eye rather than the speck in our brother's eye....and pluck it out. God encourages us to choose the path of love, peace, joy and truth rather than the path of hate, anxiety, anger and lies which comes from evil. Evil is always angry and cunning, sly and envious, plotting and malicious, jealous and unappreciative. Evil makes us proud and haughty, self-serving and unloving. Evil creates racism, justification, self importance and a blind eye to sin. But righteousness makes us happy and honest, open and supportive, appreciative and humble, giving and loving. Righteousness removes fear and hate and replaces it with peace and love. Righteousness causes us to esteem others higher than ourselves and to desire to spurn sinful actions.

Sometimes we may wish that we were a different flower in God's garden, but *we must remember that we **are** one of God's flowers. We must remember that God asks that we **appreciate where He placed us and work toward perfecting what we have been given.*** God gave us our personal attributes because He plans to use them in His new kingdom. He wants us to develop what He gave us and become the best we can. Through God, through our appreciative heart *and the **acknowledgement and forgiveness of sin,*** we can find righteousness and joy…. and satisfaction no matter where we are planted.

All gifts await us as the Bride of Christ because each of us will be a part of the garden God planted. Just as a flower will balk at being planted in a less than perfect environment, we may think that we are not where we should be. But we must remember that God never makes a mistake. What He has created is perfect and has a purpose and a place. But what Satan does is imperfect, it is evil and will in time decay. Evil is destructive and has no long term value where what God does always has long term value and a blessing always comes from God's actions.

Therefore, we need to learn that wherever we are, God will help us and draw us to our fullest potential. We have been *perfectly* created, *perfectly* planted, *perfectly* nourished and through His love and care we can grow stronger right wherever God places us. **If we seek to know and exercise God's statutes, our *happiness will not be tied to material possessions, beauty, talent, or the temporal, but tied only to the heart and the amount and purity of the love it holds.***

Let us not be those who listen to the whispers of Satan and weaken and die in sin and arrogance, but let us grow into those who develop godly strength so we can increase our faith and love to bloom in the Son!

> "Be sober, be vigilant, because your adversary the devil, as a roaring lion, walketh about, seeking who he may devour."
> 1 Peter 5:8

Chapter Seven

TAKE THIS CUP FROM ME

Our response to physical pain is easy to understand, but our response to the emotional pain which accompanies all we go through is just as difficult to bear. Sadly, we often try to hide our emotional pain from others; perhaps because we feel embarrassed to admit to emotional pain and justified to admit to physical pain. For some it might be because scripture tells us in Romans 8:28, *"All things work together for the good of those that love the Lord,* and therefore we think that we must wear a happy face regardless of how or why we suffer inside. However, those words teach us that children of God are aware that while Satan revels in both our physical and emotional heartache, **our Heavenly Father** in His loving kindness and the righteousness under which He works, desires to **turn our heartaches into a blessing**. Because we sin, our Heavenly Father has ordained that our lives be our training ground whereby we learn how to become all that God wants in those He is developing for His new kingdom. That is an incredible calling and also a difficult one when we must battle the enemy of our soul!

God allows our difficult circumstances because they can become a marker for the development of our character. Even knowing this however, there are times when we live through heartache or witness the heartache of those we love, that **we ask ourselves how this promise of good from all circumstances could be possible.** Even though we believe that scripture is God's personal, accurate and irrefutable instruction, seldom do we think to ask God to unravel the mystery attached to His words and help us recognize their miracle. *We seldom tell our Heavenly Father that we sometimes struggle to understand how to apply His words.* Thus, we suffer in silence and do not admit that inwardly we rail at what we face and then feel guilty about our private thoughts. However, as we examine scripture, we begin to learn that we are too hard on ourselves and that God understands and wants to help us.

What scripture really says about the expression of the fear, or pain, or sorrow we experience is best understood as we examine what Christ lived through and what *He* felt and expressed during His most difficult moments. Christ's words to His Father can become our example. When Christ prayed over the circumstances with which He was about to engage, Christ spoke the words, *"Take away this cup from me".* This tells us that Christ feared what He would go through and wanted God to remove it. Therefore we should not feel guilty if we wish, or ask God, to change our circumstances.

The love in Christ's heart and **the trust He had in His Father allowed Him to submit** to the sacrifice He made for us even though He feared it and wished that He would not have to endure it. As He prayed and spoke in complete honestly about His feelings, His love for His Father and for us brought forth the character in His soul which caused Him to utter the words, *"Nevertheless, not what I will, but what thou will"* immediately following His first words.

This is our example, and from it we know with certainty that God allows us to express our fear and the pain we feel, and even to wish that our circumstances were different. It is not that we are judged and found lacking if we ask God to take our troubles away, but that we **end up *accepting*** God's will and doing our best to use those circumstances to prove our character. Our troubles will then become an indicator of the trust and acceptance which has developed in our heart in regard to the decisions of our Heavenly Father....no matter what the circumstances. **How we handle our troubles becomes, in essence, a marker of our spiritual maturity and a marker of our faith.**

The miracle which occurs for each of us during these encounters with God is that when we adjust our thoughts and actions to submit to God's will, our heartaches become easier to bear. In fact, sometimes they simply disappear because once Satan realizes that he cannot break our faith, nor break our trust in God, nor make us sin, when we encounter such difficulties there is no reason for him to continue his harassment. We can therefore be released from Satan's captivity because **we have demonstrated that we are wiser and more trustworthy for having mastered the test which these circumstances brought. We have exercised our faith...we have proven our faith both to us and to our Heavenly Father!**

Certainly it is difficult to experience heartache. Whether it comes from the death of a child, a debilitating disease, a devastating betrayal, fear, watching someone we love suffer, or something else, we should examine Christ's plea that God remove the cup from which He was to drink. Then as we examine these verses further, and read Christ's words of submission, we begin to understand what this effort cost Him. We then appreciate His sacrifice and understand that what we suffer is so much less. We also realize that, while Christ's sacrifice benefitted us rather than Him, our suffering *will* benefit us personally.

Mark 14:34 tells us of the emotional pain Christ suffered: *"My soul is exceedingly sorrowful unto death."* Mark 14:36 tells us that when Christ prayed, He said, *"Abba Father, all things are possible unto thee. **Take away this cup from me**, nevertheless not* *what I will but what thou will."* What few of us realize is that Christ later **repeated** this plea. Asking God a second time and a third time to remove what was to happen was indicative of how much He was suffering as He thought about what had to be done. For Christ, this was the worst **emotional** pain possible. Mark 14:39 tells us, *"and **again He** went away and prayed, and spoke the same words."*

Therefore, if we are caught up in a circumstance which seems to have no end, we need not feel guilty when we ask God to let our circumstances pass..... as long as our heart truly desires that God's will be paramount. Such a response is indicative of the trust we place in God's design for our lives; the faith we have in Him. Further, by trying to be more introspective and asking ourselves if we **trust that what is occurring is for our good**, as scripture teaches, and if we are willing to endure our circumstances in order to develop our character, we **can** grow into those God desires to be with Him for all eternity.

Once we reflect on these questions and ask our Heavenly Father to help us learn from everything we experience, we can move with all our heart and with great sincerity from the words *"Take this away"* to the words, *"Thy will be done"*. This allows God access to our hearts and the ability to create the change in us that we require. **Our character.....which is comprised of our ability to love and forgive, to have compassion and understanding, to be honest and loyal, to submit to God's will, to trust God implicitly..... will be measured by how we deal with our circumstances. These actions honor God and honoring God is how we worship Him.**

John 4:23 tells us: *"But the hour is coming, and now is, when the true worshippers will worship the Father in spirit and truth; for **the Father is seeking such** to worship Him."* This clearly tells us that God is seeking those souls who will work to learn His truths, His words, and follow them as best they can. Those who have developed these attributes of faith will be a part of the five wise, and not the five foolish virgins, and found worthy to go with the Lord when He returns.

Our suffering, and our trials and tribulations, are always for our greater good. How we handle them will be an example to those around us. *How we approach adversity is a marker of our spiritual maturity.* These are but a few of the blessings which God creates from our heartache and why all things work for the good of those who love the Lord. Christ dreaded the circumstances which He was to live through. He was afraid. He found Himself without any earthly support, and without a true and loyal friend.

Christ's cup was a bitter one; it was the most bitter cup of circumstances we could imagine, yet because of His love for us and for His Father, He stood firm in His faith and in His love and He trusted and obeyed what His Heavenly Father ordained. Satan threw everything he had against Christ, but Christ remained stedfast. Thus, the Bride of Christ must remain firm in her trust and obedience to God and bring her sorrow and fear to God with openness and honesty. What Christ did and what He went through to complete His task should never be taken lightly. He suffered because He loves us and God allowed His Son's suffering to create an eternity for all of us which will be completely free of sorrow and of evil.

We must remember that it is okay to tell our Heavenly Father that we are tired, that we feel saddened by our circumstances, that we feel that we can no longer carry our cross. He understands and even feels sorrow for our circumstances. He knows however that our spiritual growth depends on our understanding His words and His goals and making them ours. Our spiritual growth is also dependent upon our experiences...both happy and sad. These are our greatest teachers and these build our faith.

God knows that we will be faced with a choice....good or evil.....and must make that choice using our individual free will. It is our experiences with both good and evil which will help us make that choice. It is through the evil we witness that we can appreciative what is good and can develop the desire to want to live in an environment forever which does not allow evil to exist.

The bottom line is that God loves us; He sees our tears and carries us through all circumstances. Like a parent, he wants to give us everything... every joy possible.... but **He knows what we need to mature. God wants us to** grow into the kind of person who will *choose* to live in harmony, in love, and with honor for all eternity. And sadly, we cannot appreciate these without learning what evil does to the heart and soul.

When we finally understand God's Plan of Salvation and can marvel at what He has done to bring us this incredible opportunity, we find it easier to walk in righteousness, to spurn what Satan offers and to turn our face toward the path God wants us to take. It makes is so much easier for us to accept His ways and accept His will for our lives. And as we strive, God always creates a blessing from our experiences and we gain not only godly wisdom, but also the ability to thwart what Satan tries to do to us.

Our concept of time makes it seem as if a lifetime is a long time. But in God's concept of time, a lifetime is but a blink of an eye. An eternity with God well worth the little bit of effort it takes to learn God's words and make an informed decision. As our faith grows our anxieties diminish.

> "My people are destroyed for lack of knowledge; because thou hast rejected knowledge, I will also reject thee....."
>
> Hosea 4:6

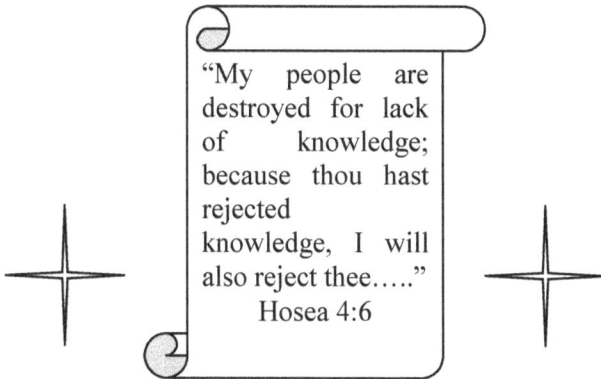

Chapter Eight

GOD'S PLAN OF SALVATION

God has a created a plan for developing mankind into those who will appreciate goodness; those who will desire to be free of all things evil and who will love one another. His plan has a beginning and an end...and we are living near its end. When God's Plan of Salvation is completed, a bride for His Son and inhabitants for His new kingdom will have been developed. The plan is specific and is open to everyone who was ever conceived, born or died.

Sadly, few understand the immensity and importance of what they have been offered through God's plan for mankind. Many will not be prepared for the day when that offer and the grace it provides is no longer available and as scripture tells us, there will be the "gnashing of teeth" in the agony this will cause. Therefore we must begin to explore what God offers and learn about the new kingdom He plans. He will fill that kingdom with souls who understand the value of love, trust, honesty and loyalty, and who will choose to practice these attributes voluntarily through their free will. Those who qualify for God's new kingdom will truly love God, and His Son, and all those whom God has chosen to share that kingdom.

To put His plan into effect, God created this temporary earth in its limited universe. He created Adam and Eve to be the first souls who would be given the opportunity to develop into those who would appreciate, and seek, the purity of love which allows the special relationships God desires to flourish. However, when God announced His plan for mankind, the beautiful and powerful angel Lucifer, later known as Satan, rebelled against God. Lucifer could not bear the fact that mankind would be elevated above the angels who held the same position he himself held. Lucifer had already become jealous of Christ, and of the position Christ held by sitting at the right hand of God. When he also became jealous of the new being which God wanted to bring to fruition, his jealousy brought him to rebellion and he gathered supporters to his cause and waged war against God. The result was that Lucifer was thrown to earth with the angels who joined his rebellion. These numbered one third of all the angels. When Lucifer was thrown out of heaven he became known as Satan.

Satan fully understood God's plan and also understood that when God's Plan of Salvation was completed and God obtained the number of faithful loving souls He longs for, Satan and his followers would be thrown into hell for the evil they brought against God and mankind. Therefore, to prevent God's plan from moving forward and thus forestall his destruction, Satan destroyed God's relationship of trust and loyalty with Adam and Eve by enticing them to sin through disobedience. Satan knew that this would force God to banish Adam and Eve as he had banished Satan. But God, knowing what Satan would do to Adam and Eve, had already provided a way for them and the generations to follow, to escape the captivity Satan proposed for them. God would teach mankind how to return to God by teaching them the difference between good and evil and showing them that they could freely choose God's way of love, and spurn Satan's way of hate.

WHAT IS FAITH?

To pay the price or the "ransom" for the sins which man would commit under Satan's influence, Christ offered Himself as the perfect sacrifice by which these sins could be forgiven. Therefore, Satan dedicated himself to interfering with God's plan, trying to break the faith and goodness of those who would follow God. Satan knew that when God collected the number of souls He wanted for His new creation, he and the angels who had rebelled with him would be bound forever. Thus **Satan is fighting for his continued freedom when discouraging the faithful.** But through God's love, many of those who would be attacked by Satan would be strengthened through these tests, becoming like gold refined in the fires of tribulation. It is from these faithful that God is building what the Bible calls the Bride of Christ.

God also provided for those who died in sin by creating a means of testimony in eternity, but this provision only lasts while grace is still available on earth. When Christ triumphed over death on the cross, He entered Hades for three days to give testimony of His triumph to those who had died in their sins before Christ brought His perfect sacrifice. While in Hades, Christ told these unredeemed souls that now they too could find forgiveness through grace if they would but seek it with a truly repentant heart.

God has allotted a certain amount of time for His children to be made ready. Only He knows when that time frame will end. (Matthew 24:36; Acts 1:7) When that time is up, Christ, His Son will leave Heaven and return to earth to take the faithful back to heaven with Him. This event is termed the First Resurrection and only those from eternity who have obtained forgiveness and those alive who are faithful will take part in this event. (James 1:18; 1 John 5:4; Revelation 2:7, 11, 26; Revelation 3:5, 12, 21, Revelation 12:5 and 11; Revelation 21:7) When they are gone, grace as we know it, will be removed from the earth and no longer available to those who remain, and a great destruction will begin where one third of all the people on earth will die. (Daniel 12:1-2; Matthew 24:21-22; Thessalonians 2:1-4; 2 Timothy 3:1-9)

Three and one half years after these souls have been removed from the earth, the destruction will end and God will send His Son back to earth with those He had taken at the First Resurrection. The souls who were taken earlier will have celestial (perfect) bodies and will reign as kings and priests for one thousand years of peace when they will bring testimony to everyone living or dead who were not taken in the First Resurrection. Satan will be bound during this time, unable to influence mankind, so all mankind will learn about... **and accept...** God's offer to become all that is required of them. (Revelation20:2; Isaiah4:2-6; Isaiah 11; Isaiah 12; Daniel 2:44; Daniel 7:27; Amos 9:11-15) Those who receive this testimony will not have the opportunity to become a part of the Bride of Christ because the Bride was formed from those who Christ had taken at the First Resurrection. But **these remaining souls will be given the opportunity to become an inhabitant of God's new kingdom**.

After the one thousand years of peace and perfect testimony, Satan will be loosed again for a little while so those who accept God's offer during this time period can be tested. (Revelation 20:7-10) Satan, knowing that his time is almost up will wreak havoc on those not firm in their faith and many will fall. Then will come Judgment Day (John 5:22; Revelation 20:12-14) when everyone, *except* those taken by Christ for the First Resurrection, **will be judged** by what they did or did not do during their lifetime. Those who were taken by Christ at the First Resurrection will reign as kings and priests in the new kingdom. They will never have to be judged because their sins had been forgiven and entirely wiped away by God. But those who were not taken at that time, yet received testimony during the thousand years of peace, *will* face judgment.

Scripture tells us that this judgment will separate the "goats" from the "lambs". The "goats," are those who will not accept God's statutes, those who were unrepentant for bringing harm to God's children, those who mocked God will be cast into hell with Satan forever. This is called the second death and it is torment for all eternity. But others, those called the "lambs," those who remained faithful to God's words after the testimony they accepted during the thousand years of peace, will live outside the City Gates where the Royal Family of God will reside but will inhabit God's new kingdom where there will be no sorrow and no tears. (Revelation 21:1-4) In the end, only those who did their best to learn and do God's will and developed in love will share God's new heaven and earth. **The goats, along with all evil and all hate will be bound forever with Satan and his demons, never to harm God's children again.** (Revelation 21:1-4)

To sum this up, a specific amount of time has been allotted in God's Plan of Salvation for His chosen ones to be made ready. (Acts 1:6-7) When that time is up, God will send His Son back to earth for the First Resurrection (Revelation 20:5) when He will take to heaven both those from eternity who have obtained forgiveness and those alive who have remained faithful. (11 Peter 3:10) When they are gone, grace will also be gone, and the final destruction of the end times will begin on the earth where, among other things, **one-third of all the people on earth will die and the rest will long for death.**

When the destruction ends, God will send His Son back to earth with those He had taken at the First Resurrection who had been given celestial (perfect) bodies. They will reign with Christ as kings and priests for one thousand years and bring testimony to everyone living or dead who was not taken in the First Resurrection. Satan will be bound during this time, unable to influence mankind, so all will learn about and accept God. But, after the one thousand years of peace, Satan will be loosed again for a little while so those who received testimony and accepted God can be tested. (Revelation 20:7) Satan will wreak havoc on those not firm in their faith and many will fall and follow Satan again. (Revelation 20:2)

Then the Day of Judgment will arrive when everyone will be judged, *except* those taken by Christ in the First Resurrection. Those who accept Christ and remain faithful after Satan is loosed again, scripture calls the "lambs", and they will be allowed to occupy the new heaven God is creating. But those who did not accept Christ, had no remorse for the harm they did, or fell to Satan again when he was loosed, scripture calls the "goats", and they will be cast into hell with Satan and the fallen angels and tormented day and night forever. (Revelation 20:10 and 15) Those taken in the First Resurrection will reign with Christ in the new kingdom and never have to be judged because their sins were forgiven, and entirely wiped away by God.

Heaven rejoices in these who remained faithful to God from the beginning. These souls are the specific number of souls which scripture refers to as the firstfruits, and as the Bride of Christ. These souls are also mentioned in the Apocrypha. 11 Esdras 2:40-41 says, *"Receive they number O Sion, and embrace those of thine that are clothed in white which have fulfilled the law of the Lord.* **The number of thy children whom thou longest for, is fulfilled:** *beseech the Lord that thy people, which have been called from the beginning, may be hallowed."* Jude 1:6 tells us: *"And **the angels which kept not their first estate, but left their own habitation, he hath reserved in everlasting chains** under darkness unto the judgment of the great day,"*

What we must remember is that Satan loves the anonymity of working in secret to keep us from God. He wants us to hate, to judge, to condemn, to be complacent, to think that we know better than scripture, and to bask in our own limited understanding. Satan is so subtle that many cannot believe that he exists, or that his fallen angels have the power to bring such harm to mankind. Genesis 3:1 tells us, *"..... the serpent was more subtil than any beast......"* Scripture teaches us that Satan is a liar, a murderer (of men's souls), and is subtle in his attacks, and that he walks this earth to influence mankind. Matthew 4:1 adds that Satan also tempts us and calls him "the tempter". *"Then was Jesus led...... to be tempted of the devil."* And in Matthew 4: 3 *"and when the tempter came to Him, he said....."*

Thus we know that Satan has power, is unscrupulous, and wants to separate us from God; we know that the fallen angels who work with Satan also tempt and lie and are subtle in their attacks. We also know that Satan is fully aware of the prophecies of scripture; he knows his own end and knows what he must do to delay the day when he is to be bound. Satan and his fallen angels work at a feverish pitch during these end times because they too know the signs which depict that soon Christ will return.

Satan's work revolves around his need to delay the completion of God's Plan of Salvation. With every soul God brings in, Satan works in the hope of causing one to fall away. But God, knowing man would sin, arranged for him to learn of good and evil so he would have the opportunity to recognize the wiles of Satan, freely choose good, repent of all evil, and thereby seek the forgiveness of sin. As God blesses His children they gather closely and long for their new life with God when evil will no longer plague them.

God will fill His kingdom with souls who will truly love *one another*, and love His Son and Him above all else. God's Plan of Salvation will be completed despite what Satan does, and Satan and his fallen angels and all evil will one day be bound and God's new kingdom will emerge. The question then remains, "On which side will we be?"

Scripture warns that we are not to trust our own understanding because it is so limited and so easily influenced by Satan. It teaches us that we must trust God's words and follow His statutes to escape what Satan can do. Proverbs 3:5-7 says: *"Trust in the Lord with all your heart and lean not unto thine own understanding. In all ways acknowledge Him and He shall make thy paths. **Be not wise in thine own eyes....**"*

And God also tells us how we are to conduct ourselves. Philippians 4:8 says: *"Finally brethren, whatever things are true, whatever things are noble, whatever things are just, whatever things are pure, whatever things are lovely, whatever things are of good report, if there is any virtue and if there is anything praiseworthy--meditate on these things."*

We will fail; we will continue to make mistakes, we will continue to be disappointed in ourselves, and in others, but if we strive, if we seek forgiveness and forgive others, if we have remorse for those failures, and desire to please God, he will always be at our side. God will build our faith and He will make us worthy when Christ returns. God looks directly into our heart where we cannot hide the true person we are. If He finds that we love Him, seek Him, desire to love others, try to give of ourselves, follow His statutes as best we can, He will forgive the mistakes we make. But to do this we must know God's words, know what He asks of us and why, know His Plan of Salvation and desire to be a part of it with all our heart. That is the beginning of faith.

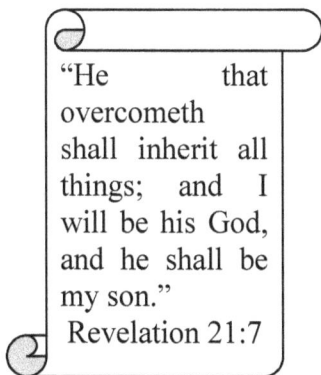

> "He that overcometh shall inherit all things; and I will be his God, and he shall be my son."
> Revelation 21:7

Chapter Nine

FAILURE FROM WITHIN

Scripture warns that false doctrines will abound in the time just before Christ returns, and that this may come "from within" or by "those among us".... yet we seldom examine what is closest to us. We look at other churches, other doctrines, and other leaders without considering that **this powerful warning must also be applied to the circles in which we personally travel.** The strength of this admonition is evidenced by its similar words in other passages throughout the Bible. Scripture tells us that God Himself inspired the words of the Bible by sending His Holy Spirit to work in the heart of those who wrote, translated and published this incredible Book. In creating the Bible the Holy Spirit of God worked through two kings (David and Solomon), two priests (Jeremiah and Ezekiel), one physician (Luke), two fishermen (Peter and John), two shepherds (Moses and Amos), one Pharisee and theologian (Paul), one statesman (Daniel), one tax collector (Matthew), one soldier (Joshua), one scribe (Ezra), one butler (Nehemiah), and others. This teaches us that no matter what our station in life, God is available to us and loves us and finds value in us.

All scripture is the Divine Word of our living God, thus what we see and hear in this world must be compared to what scripture tells us. We are told to heed its words. And we are warned in Revelation 22:18-19: *"if any man shall take away from the words of the book of this prophecy, **God shall take away his part out of the book of life,** and out of the holy city, and from the things which are written in this book".* Scripture also transcends time and culture and is a book for all ages, for all of mankind, and to be especially heeded for these end times even when we do not fully understand everything God wrote . 2 Timothy 3:15-16 tells us: *"And that from a child thou hast known **the holy scriptures, which are able to make thee wise unto salvation**........All scripture **is given by inspiration of God,** and is profitable for doctrine, for reproof, for correction, **for instruction in righteousness**".*

However, Satan, in his effort to delay the completion of God's plan, works to separate man from God by encouraging us to sin, encouraging us to condone sin in others, and to encourage our arrogance to think that we do not need to trust scripture as the word of God. Satan's goal is to cause us to take the words of scripture out of context and point us to those passages which can easily be misinterpreted. He does not want us to heed the words of Christ nor the words of the early Apostles which teach us to uncover sin, rebuke sin, and exhort our brothers and sisters to worthily seek the grace which Christ provided. Grace is free to everyone regardless of one's past. But obtaining grace requires us to *acknowledge* **our sins and strive to** *overcome them.*

We are also asked to bring testimony of this redemptive work to others thereby furthering God's work and helping to bring God's Plan of Salvation to its completion. We are to share what we learn about God's words with others....and *"lean not unto our own understanding".* Because there may be a few chapters or verses in scripture which are not easily understood, some allow these to keep them from believing *any* of the words of scripture. One example of this is found in Leviticus which atheists point to as authenticating slavery. But here God was explaining that in any era and circumstance every one of us might find ourselves enslaved; by people; by governments; by dictators; by poverty, by sin; by a lack of education; even by our own arrogance or complacency and that regardless of our circumstances, God will help us thrive. Other non-believers quote Deuteronomy as a chapter which gives permission to sell our children into slavery and yet God is teaching us that He can bring us *out* of *any* **bondage** no matter what circumstances brought us there. Joseph was sold into slavery by his brothers but God used that circumstance to elevate Joseph and allow him to help his family and his people during a time of drought and famine.

Some unbelievers have even said that the Sermon on the Mount condones the sins prevalent in today's society while in truth it is in this sermon that Christ asks us to fulfill *every* commandment and to follow **all** of God's statutes. In fact, when Christ healed those who came to him and forgave their sins, he often ended His interaction with them by saying: *"Go, and sin no more"*. This and other passages teach us that while grace is freely offered, **forgiveness carries the pre-requisite that we seek out and acknowledge our sins, have remorse for them, desire not to commit them again and forgive others.**

There are also those who negate some parts of scripture yet believe other parts. They may believe that Christ has the power to forgive our sins but not that anything is required of them to obtain that forgiveness. They may accept that we have a soul which will live forever, but not that when God's Plan of Salvation is completed **our soul must live on in only one of three places: The City of God, the Kingdom of God or the Lake of Fire.** Some may feel that the fallibility of the Bible lies in the proof of carbon dating. Yet in Genesis we learn that the sun and moon... which provided us with our first 24 hour "day" .....were not created until the end of the 4th day. This would certainly allow for the prior "days" to be that time period which had **no time reference** that our limited intelligence can understand thus allowing for carbon dating and even for evolution. In fact, in these verses God tells us that when He created the animals for our era, they would come forth only of their "own kind" which tells us that no further evolution would take place. There are many such facts found in scripture.

Another example is in the medical studies which have demonstrated the Bible's perfect accuracy. The combination of safety factors regarding blood clotting and the immune system found in the blood of a mother and newborn child dictate that circumcision is **safest for the child** on the eighth day after birth. This shows us what God provided for mankind in regard to his health.... and what man did not know.... when God told the Israelites to circumcise their male children on the eighth day of life.

Further, modern science has shown us the danger of eating pork in conditions where there is no proper refrigeration. Thus the Bible warns the Israelites not to eat pork at that time. Yet scripture also points out that God had the power to modify this danger when it relates the story of the Apostle authorized by God to eat the pork served by the soldier. In these stories God again shows us His knowledge and power and protection. There are many such incidents described throughout scripture.

The Bible clearly teaches us what sin is in God's eyes; that God never changes; and that what God deems a sin remains a sin and taints the soul....unless that sin is forgiven. For us, in the here and now, we understand that Christ teaches us that we must not judge because we cannot know what a soul has been through, nor know the circumstances which might lead a soul to sin. However, the Bible tells us that we must "teach, rebuke, and exhort" what we have learned of God's words **and exercise** the four pre-requisites for obtaining the forgiveness of sin. These are that sins can be forgiven only *if they are acknowledged as a sin, if we have remorse for having committed them, if we honestly desire to overcome them, and if we forgive others.*

2 Timothy 4:2 teaches: "Preach the word, be instant in season, out of season; reprove, rebuke, exhort, with all long suffering and doctrine." Yet, despite these words we see that in today's world

of "political correctness" Satan has obtained an incredibly powerful platform even amongst churches, ministers, teachers and politicians and has blinded men to the truth. His cunning today is amazingly similar to the words he used with Adam and Eve when he insinuated....*"surely God didn't mean....."*. The cajoling words of political correctness claim that some cannot help the sins they commit, others say that what the Bible calls sin is not sin after all, and admonish us to "be compassionate" as if we are not.

Political correctness demands that we not judge *thus must allow....even condone.....* sin. Political correctness, inspired by Satan has also lobbied for laws which condemn thus immobilize those who provide spiritual insight into what God tells us *is* sin. 2 Corinthians 11:14 clearly warns: *"Believe not every spirit for Satan masquerades as an angel of light".* Yet scripture, while it does tell us not to judge, does *not* tell us that we must allow or condone sin. In fact, the Bible teaches us to love the sinner....**rebuke the sin... and exhort the sinner to overcome** their sin.

Adam and Eve meant well. They did not set out to destroy their relationship with God. They were drawn into disobeying God because of the subtle and well worded argument Satan brought them. The same ploy is being used today to make us wonder if indeed, scripture could be wrong, if God *really* means it when He terms a sin an abomination; if He *really* demands acknowledgement of those things which many feel they cannot resist. Sadly, the satanic words of political correctness imply that God does *not* mean that those engaged in these sins will **really** be kept from being a part of the new heaven and earth. They imply that the Bible's description of God's rules are unfair...and thus not what God *really* wants. They speak of Christ's forgiving heart but conveniently ignore what **the sacrament of Holy Communion demands.** 1 Corinthians 11:27-29 warns: *"Wherefore whosoever shall eat this bread and drink this cup of the Lord, **unworthily** shall be guilty.......But let a man examine himself.....For he that* *eateth and drinketh unworthily, eateth and drinketh damnation to himself...."*

While God wants all men saved; He clearly states that no sin or sinful nature can enter His new Heaven and Earth. God tells us right up front that His Plan of Salvation was instituted into the physics of our world to separate good from evil for all eternity and that all evil.....**by His standards**.... will be bound in the Lake of Fire. God wants us to understand that our sojourn on earth and the free will God gave us *is the righteousness under which God has chosen to labor* so that **Satan can never say that God manipulated the choice we make between good and evil.** If we truly love God and want to be a part of His new kingdom, we automatically come to hate our sin *even when we cannot break free* of it. When we love someone we do not want to disappoint them....we want to please them. When we learn about sin, we also learn why it is not good for us and why **it will not be allowed to enter the new kingdom. Sin cannot be forgiven if one scoffs at the word of God which identifies those sins.** Thus we are to teach.... as a church... as ministers..... as a people... as children of God... that we are *not* to condone sin of any kind. Yet we are to love the sinner and in that love, teach the sinner that if they truly love God and have remorse for having disappointed Him, they can obtain forgiveness ....if they willingly acknowledge their sins and *desire* to sin no more... even if they fail over and over again.

The bottom line is that we must love all people, all sinners; that we must care, must teach even if this means that we must rebuke out of that love *__and be condemned for doing so__*. We must welcome all sinners into our midst and pray with them and for them. But *__if we condone one another's sins, we are just as guilty of that sin as they are.__* We contribute to the arrogance of their soul when we support the continuation of their sin. When we do this we have allowed the "wolves to enter amongst us" and to **dictate a new set of rules about what God considers sin** and how we can obtain forgiveness! We too can then lose our soul salvation. It may not be popular or politically correct to stand by God's rules, but it is the only way to truly love God and love others enough to want to bring them the truth. It is the understanding and accepting of God's will; the love we develop for God that **makes us want to overcome** our sins, and it is the *striving* heart that God looks for....not the *failures.*

As long as we get back up after falling, brush ourselves off, and thrust our chin out with determination to **"go and sin no more"** we will have God's help and forgiveness! God loves the valiant warrior even if he trips over his own feet from time to time! **God's plan offers us the sacraments He has provided for mankind which allows them to sidestep the repercussion of the inherited sin produced by Adam and Eve and also their personal sins....and enter once again into fellowship with God.** And God loves those who help others find forgiveness and salvation.

A sacrament, or covenant with God, contains certain rules for receiving the gifts which are offered to us and are designed to re-open the door to a relationship with God which was lost when Adam and Eve sinned. **Holy Baptism, Holy Communion, and Holy Sealing are the three sacraments which have the power to re-institute mans' access to God.** They are the prerequisites for an invitation into the new kingdom which God is establishing for those who love Him. The sin of Adam and Eve destined man to experience evil. Once evil entered the heart of Adam and Eve, access to God was denied not only to them but to the generations to follow.

The sacraments, however, re-open those doors allowing us access to God and also brings us God's protection. They are to help us escape the consequences of our sins **and** the influence of the sins of our forefathers. Remaining in sin brings dire consequences to our soul and will be rampant during the end times. Scripture describes the conditions of the world when Christ returns and tells us that many will be so engaged in their daily activities that they will be taken unaware and will be unprepared when the moment arrives. Matthew 25:40-42 tells us *"Then shall two be in the field; the one shall be taken, and the other left. Two women* *shall be grinding at the mill, the one shall be taken, and the other left. Watch therefore; **for ye know not what hour your Lord doth come.**"* These verses indicate that only **half of those who believe** will be ready. Matthew 25:10-13 tells us: *"....they that **were ready** went in with him.....and **the door was shut.** Afterward came also the other virgins, saying, Lord, Lord, open to us. But he answered and said, Verily I say unto you, I know ye not. Watch therefore for you know neither the day nor the hour wherein the Son of man cometh."*

There are many parables and much instruction throughout scripture which tells us that God has asked *all* men to make themselves ready for the return of Christ by learning of Him and striving to do as He asks. God desires that *all* men be saved and **He brings testimony to _everyone in one form or another_.** But as we read these parables and the words of the Apostles, we learn that though many are called, many **will not** accept God's invitation and will put forth a variety of reasons to justify **why** they will not. Some are "too busy", some think they know better than what scripture teaches, some refuse full knowledge about God, some are so filled with hatred that they bring harm to the messengers of God, some take pride in their own intelligence, and others fall into a state of complacency about spiritual matters.

Scripture warns us that no one knows when Christ will return. Matthew 24:36 tells us, *"But of that day and hour **knoweth no man**...but my Father only."* We also read that those who will be left behind will be in great agony. Matthew 22:13 says, *".... **there shall be weeping and gnashing of teeth.**"* Scripture also tells us about the signs we will see as we approach the end times. Matthew 24:4-12,24 tell us, *"....wars, rumours of wars, famine, pestilences, earthquakes in diverse places, hatred toward Christians, betrayals, hatred, false prophets with signs and wonders, iniquity, no love"* Luke 21: 25 explains, *"And there shall be signs in the sun, and in the moon, and in the stars....the sea and the waves roaring....Men's hearts failing them for fear...."* And 2 Timothy 3:1-7 tells us, *"...in the last days perilous times* *shall come. For men shall be lovers of their own selves, covetous, boasters, proud, blasphemers, disobedient to parents, unthankful, unholy. Without natural affection, trucebreakers, false accusers, incontinent, fierce, despisers of those that are good. Traitors, heady, high minded, lovers of pleasures more than lovers of God;* **Having a form of godliness but denying the power thereof....ever learning, and never able to come to the knowledge of the truth."**

And 2 Esdras 16:24 from the Apocrypha adds: *"At that time shall friends fight one against another..."* 1 Thessalonians 4:16 tells us, *"For the Lord himself shall descend from heaven with a shout....then we....shall be caught up....to meet the Lord in the air....."* 1 Thessalonians 5:2 warns: *"For yourselves know perfectly that the day of the Lord so cometh as a thief in the night."* 2 Peter 3:10, 14 tells us, *"But the day of the Lord will come as a thief in the night.....Wherefore, beloved, seeing that ye look for such things,* **be diligent that ye** *may* **be found** *of him in peace,* **without spot, and blameless."** Revelation 9:6 tells us, **"And in those days shall men seek death and shall not find it, and shall desire to die, and death shall flee from them."** Matthew 24:21, 22 warns, **"For then shall be great tribulation, such as was not since the beginning of the world to this time, no, nor ever shall be.** *And except those days should be shortened, there should no flesh be saved: but for the elect's sake those days shall be shortened."*

The Bible also speaks about the "wedding feast" which is the place in heaven where the Bride of Christ will be taken when Christ returns for them. This event will last for three and one half years while the horrors of evil work upon the earth and the satanic demons are unleashed against mankind and.... **there is no grace to cover man's failures.** After this time elapses, Christ and those He took at the First Resurrection will return to earth to bring testimony to all who had once spurned His teachings. Satan and his cohorts will be bound during this testimony therefore everyone **will** accept God's offer.

But then evil will be loosed again to test those who newly receive Christ's testimony. After this will come judgment where *everything* that is evil will be exposed and then bound *forever*. We are warned through scripture and also through a variety of venues that if we are *not* prepared we cannot expect to be part of the First Resurrection. The parable of the five wise and five foolish virgins demonstrates that only half of those who **proclaim** themselves a child of God will have the door of salvation open to them. Matthew 25:1-13 tells this parable in its entirety, but the outcome can be found in Matthew 25:11-12: "......*Lord, Lord, open up to us. But he answered and said, Verily I say unto you, 'I know you not."*

There may be very little time before we are caught up in the terrors of the end times and little time to take note of our shortcomings so we can make the necessary corrections. We are to prepare our soul as meticulously as a Bride prepares for her wedding. If we fail to do this and have not developed as God has requested, when Christ arrives for the First Resurrection, we will be rejected....although those left will still be given an opportunity to become a part of God's kingdom....**not His family, but His kingdom**.....as "lambs" after great tribulation and terrible judgment.

But for those who *are* prepared for the return of Christ, God tells us not to fear those days. He encourages us throughout scripture to be courageous. Psalm 27:14 tells us, *"Wait on the Lord: be of good courage...."* Psalm 31:24 says, *"Be of good courage, and he shall strengthen your heart...."* Isaiah 12:2 tells us, *"Behold, God is my salvation; I will trust and not be afraid...."* 11 Chronicles 19:11 states, *".....Deal courageously, and the Lord shall be with the good."* Nevertheless, there may be times when we are frightened and our tears will flow and we will suffer. But, because of what we have learned **we will know why,** and know that help is on its way. We can be comforted by God's words in Revelation 2:10: ***"Fear none of those things which thou shalt suffer...."*** And in Luke 12:32: *"Fear not, little flock; For it is your Father's good pleasure to give you the kingdom."*

If we are faithful and strive to learn of God and follow His precepts, we will experience the wonderful promise God reveals in Revelation 21:4: *"And God shall wipe away all tears from their eyes; and there shall be no more death, neither sorrow, nor crying, **neither shall there be any more pain…..**"* Matthew 25:21 comforts us with the words: *"…..thou hast been faithful over a few things, I will make thee ruler over many…"*

Faith cannot be bought and it cannot be bargained for but it is a gift for which we can work and pray. **Faith comes from knowing God's plan and believing it; trusting it.** Faith comes from trusting what we have learned from scripture and from the desire to actually become all that God wants us to become. Hebrew 10:23-25 tells us: *"Let us **hold fast the profession of our faith without wavering**: (for he is faithful that promised:) And let us consider one another to provoke unto love and to good works. Not forsaking the assembling of ourselves together, as the manner of some is; but exhorting one another: and so much the more, as ye see the day approaching.*

These words tell us to continue to learn God's words, share them with one another, and invite others to hear them. We are to support one another whenever we waver and encourage one another to work toward the day of Christ's return. We must keep our faith alive and ask God to increase our faith. Scripture clearly warns that the end times will bring the entire world so much heartache that many, even the children of God will wonder if God hears them; even if there really is a God who cares for them. Therefore, we have to develop our faith now so we can withstand those times.

Revelation 14:15 reminds us of the moment God tells Christ to fetch His bride with the words: *"….Thrust in thy sickle and reap; for the time is come for thee to reap; for the harvest of the earth is ripe."* That will be a day of rejoicing for many, but also a day of terrible remorse for those who, like the five foolish virgins, believed that they would be taken and were not. Sadly, at that point, it's too late and at the most these souls can still work toward becoming a "lamb" in God's kingdom when the Day of Judgment arrives. Sadly, once grace is removed from the earth, this becomes harder to do and Satan becomes more frenzied in his hatred against those who love God. The destruction which the Bible describes will be terrible and will make men want to die rather than live through it.

Faith begins with a desire to share in the future God offers and can blossom into one of the most powerful and protective forces imaginable. However, we must also remember that **our faith will be tested and we will have to be firmly rooted in God's words to withstand that test.** Knowing God, believing what He says and seeking to obey His statutes will keep us strong. When we have passed that test and proven our faith, God's reward will be ours. Romans 15:4 reminds us *"For whatsoever things were written aforetime were written **for our learning**, that we through patience and comfort **of the scripture** might have hope.*

Romans 14:22 tells us: *Hast thou faith? have it to thyself before God....."* And in Hebrews 11:1 we learn: *"Now faith is the substance of things hoped for, the evidence of things not seen."* And in Hebrew 11: 6 we can read: *"But without faith it is impossible to please him....."*

"And they that shall be wise shall shine as the brightness of the firmament; and they that turn many to righteousness as the stars for ever and ever."

Daniel 12:3

Chapter Ten

THE BENEFITS OF FAITH

When we open our heart to God and learn about His Plan of Salvation we also learn about God's incredibly loving nature. His love for us is evident through the marvelous future He wants to provide for us. Once we fully understand the scope of God's plan, each of us cannot help but desire to participate in such a magnificent end result. From this, we also learn the purpose of our life, and the reason for sorrow. We learn why we fail to do that which we want to do and why we do instead those things we wish we didn't. We learn why relationships become strained and what causes this. We understand why our suffering is often the best form of instruction and can therefore be a blessing. We also begin to see how each part of scripture contributes to the whole. Hebrews 1:14 tells us: *Are they not all ministering spirits, sent to minister for them, who shall receive the inheritance of salvation?"*

As our faith grows in what God has so carefully laid out for us, so does our assurance that there is nothing which can occur in our life that God has not allowed. We see how God uses every circumstance we go through for our edification. As we learn to trust this truth, we develop the ability to endure our hardships with nobility. We understand that from those experiences, God can develop our souls and create those who will become the Bride of Christ. Therefore, we welcome the struggles we face as an opportunity to prove our loyalty and to work toward the goal of an eternity with our Heavenly Father. And finally, as we study the word of God we begin to understand why **we _must_ experience evil to appreciate righteousness** and how this will allow us to _voluntarily_ **exercise our free will to choose between good and evil. This is a choice which all of mankind will eventually make ...consciously or unconsciously**.

Because there can be _no_ evil in God's new kingdom, without our free-will consent and our desire to spurn all things evil, the rule of righteousness will not allow us to be a part of God's new kingdom. **As we search for answers and for ways to live with difficult circumstances, we also learn that it is our faith that allows us to trust God when our life is going badly.** Faith is what encourages us to pray, to believe that our prayers are heard, and to learn and grow from every trial and tribulation. Revelation 2:10 tells us: _"**Fear none of those things which thou shalt suffer**: behold the devil shall cast some of you into prison; that ye may be tried; and ye shall have tribulation ten days**: be thou faithful unto death, and I will give thee a crown of life**."_ This explains that the life of a true child of God will have its troubles but that <u>God limits the time allotted for these troubles and will give us the treasure of His kingdom when this life is over</u>.

Revelation 4:11 tells us: _Behold, I come quickly; **hold that fast** which thou hast; that no man take thy crown."_ The words "hold fast" tells us that we must work to the very end to maintain our faith. It is faith which will help us retain the crown of glory for which we have laboured. Hearing and thereby learning God's words help us in this endeavor. As mentioned earlier, Rev 3:6, 13, and 22 repeat the words: _"He that hath an ear, **let him hear** what the Spirit sayeth unto the churches......"._ By hearing what God's Plan of Salvation is all about, by asking God to open our understanding, and by availing ourselves of the sacraments God offers, we learn about God and the future He wants us to have. As we strive to overcome the temptation of sin, we align ourselves with Christ. Revelation 3:5 tells us: *"He that overcometh, the same shall be clothed in white raiment; and I will not blot out his name in the book of life, but I will confess his name before my Father, and before the angels."* And Psalm 18: 17-19 adds: *"He delivered me from my strong enemy, and from them which hated me; for they were too strong for me. They prevented me in the day of my calamity; but the Lord was my stay. He brought me forth also into a large place; he delivered me, because he delighted in me."*

Despite the hatred which Satan has for the children of God and the actions of those he sends against us, God protects us and provides angels who protect us. Scripture teaches us that love can thwart the effects of evil. The love we know as humans can be fickle and shallow while the love of God is perfect and enduring. Matthew 22:37-39 tells us: *"Jesus said unto him, Thou shalt love the Lord thy God with all thy heart, and with all thy soul, and with all thy mind. This is the first and great commandment. And the second is like unto it, Thou shalt love thy neighbor as thyself."*

Therefore we are to not only love God and the Lord Jesus, but we must also **love those whom They love**. We are to stay under the protection of God and in the fellowship of other believers to escape evil. 2 Corinthians 11:14 warns: *"And no marvel; for Satan himself is transformed into an angel of light."* Our Heavenly Father understands that as the end time prophesies are fulfilled, **the children of God will be persecuted and evil will prosper,** thus He wants us to be assured that He will care for us through these adversities. By understanding God's Plan of Salvation and knowing that our suffering is for a limited time, we can more easily **withstand the days of evil and the wiles of Satan and his fallen angels.** We can help one another when we are weak and discouraged. We can teach and exhort, we can learn and through that learning we can grow stronger in faith. God promises to help us learn if we seek Him with a pure heart.

God wants us to understand the torment that the second death will bring to sinners as opposed to the eternity of hope and joy offered to those who strive to be God's children. To help us even further, God provides us with a glimpse of the new heaven and earth not only to strengthen us but to make us aware of the incredible wonder of what He plans for us. One small example of what we will encounter in this new world can be found in the writings of the Apostle John, who, while on the island of Patmos, wrote about the streets of heaven being paved in gold, trees which will bear fruit every week, sunlight which is brighter than any ever seen before, gates made of pearls and jewels, and many other descriptions that are beyond what we can imagine.

These are analogies given to help us comprehend the immense beauty of the new creation which those who remain faithful will enjoy. While many may enter this new world, the Bride of Christ, (those taken at the First Resurrection), will live and reign at God's side. They are referred to as the "firstfruits" and also as the "overcomers", and the "kings" and "priests" of God's new world. They are a group of people, not a single person and are those who developed a close and loving relationship with their Heavenly Father and with Christ, who is referred to as the Bridegroom of their soul. To be a part of the Bride of Christ means that these souls will become the "daughter-in-law" to God and, as the culture of the days of Christ teaches, they will live in the same home which God and Christ will occupy.

Thus these words and descriptions of those Christ will take at the First Resurrection and what they will be given teach us how closely tied to God and Christ these souls will be for all of eternity. **They are, in essence promised a place in God's home....inside the gates of the City of God which will be occupied by God's "Royal Family".** The Bride of Christ are those who loved God and **demonstrated their love by learning of Him, trusting Him, and obeying Him.** While on earth, they worked on themselves, and in the vineyard to help others.... and are being rewarded for that labour. They willingly gave up the pleasures of the world to serve God and do as God asked. They did not "lean toward their own understanding" but took to heart God's words and statutes. In this new world, all evil will be bound which means that all hate, envy, prejudice, anger, back-biting, lies, plots, malice, sin, arrogance, pride and other evils will no longer plague them. It means that they will live with love, kindness, goodness, perfection, honour, righteousness, truth, beauty, health and providence for all eternity... and they will never again experience sorrow or shed tears.

Scripture tells us that when Christ takes His Bride from Earth, they will be given a celestial body which will never know sickness or death. 1 Corinthians 15:22 tells us: *"For as **in Adam all die**, even so **in Christ shall all be made alive.*** 1 Corinthians 15:35 says, *"But some man will say, How are the dead raised up? and with what body do they come? Behold, I shew you a mystery"*; and 1 Corinthians 15:51 tells us, *"We shall not all sleep, but **we shall all be changed.**"* These verses tell us that all men must die to their Adam-like nature, but that those who follow Christ will be made alive and will be changed.

When the children of God (dead and alive) are assembled to join Christ for the First Resurrection they will be transformed from their terrestrial or natural body to a celestial or spiritual body. 1 Corinthians 15:40 explains: *"There are also celestial bodies, and bodies terrestrial: but the glory of the celestial is one, and the glory of the terrestrial is another."* And 1 Corinthians 15:44 says, *"It is sown a natural body; **it is raised a spiritual body**. There is a natural body, and there is a spiritual body."* 1 Corinthians 15:47-49 tells us, *"The first man is of the earth, earthy; the second man is the Lord from heaven....And **as we have borne the image of the earthly, we shall also bear the image of the heavenly.**"*

These are incredible promises and revelations, but they also issue the warning that we must *labour* for this gift by being faithful, and by striving to learn of God and then following His statutes to the best of our ability. 1 Corinthians 15:58 tells us, *"Therefore, my beloved brethren, **be ye steadfast, <u>unmoveable</u>, always abounding in the work of the Lord**, forasmuch as ye know that your labour is not in vain of the Lord."* Psalm 1:1-3 tells us, *"Blessed is the man that walketh not in the counsel of the ungodly, nor standeth in the way of sinners, nor sitteth in the seat of the scornful. But **his delight is in the law of the Lord;** and in his law doth he meditate day and night. And he shall be like a tree planted by the rivers of water, that bringeth forth his fruit in his season; his leaf also shall not wither, and whatsoever he doeth shall prosper."*

Here we learn who God will bless and what our behavior must be to be worthy of the celestial body which will rise at the First Resurrection. Although we all must die because of Adam, in Christ we will be made alive again. Psalms 1:1 tells us: *"walketh not in the counsel of the ungodly......but **delight in the law of the Lord."*** The children of God await the return of Christ when He will take from the earth those who are worthy to become His Bride. He will choose those who have proven faithful and loving; those willing to follow God's rules of righteousness.

Thus, God's children strive to overcome the self-serving Adam-like nature and develop a Christ-like nature to achieve this goal. They understand that a loving father who seeks a bride for his son would want that bride to be kind, longsuffering, loyal and forgiving. They also know that scripture warns that only *half* of those who *are believers* will meet the criteria required to become the Bride. Therefore we must consider what will happen to those who, like the five foolish virgins, are left behind. These five foolish virgins were believers who thought they *were* prepared, but were *not* prepared for the arrival of the bridegroom. Therefore they were **not** allowed to go with Christ when He came for them. (Matthew 1:1-13, and 24:40-41)

Scripture also provides us with a description of life after death during the time before Christ came to offer the forgiveness of sin. Luke 16:19-31 provides an excellent portrayal of the place of rest for the righteous **and the place of torment for the sinner** before Christ's redemptive work was completed.   A portion of the Bride will come from those in that **"place of rest for the righteous"** who await the return of Christ. These and those who are still on earth and are found faithful will be those Christ will take. They will be deemed the "firstfruits" and the "overcomers". To be a part of the Bride of Christ is the hope of all the children of God but clearly requires the development of the Christ-like gentle nature of perfect love and goodness, and the desire to spurn *all* things evil. This then requires faith, and love, and the honest effort to be pleasing in the eyes of God. Although not all who believe *will* be found worthy to become the Bride of Christ, our Heavenly Father longs for all men to be saved and has made every provision for this to occur.

Sadly, while many will receive the invitation, few will accept. **The soul never dies, and the second death is separation from God and from love *for all eternity.*** There is *no* redemption from the second death, it is torment; it is evil; it is for all eternity; *it is forever.* These words may seem harsh but are a reminder that not all believers will be a part of the First Resurrection and become a part of the Bride of Christ and not all the souls who are left behind will remain faithful through the tribulation nor after the thousand years of peace when Satan again attacks. We need to clearly understand this truth so we will strive to shed our old nature, become more like Christ, desire to leave all things evil, learn to love, to trust God and.... teach these truths to our children.

God sees *everything* **including the hidden recesses of our heart. He knows our motives and our faults and failings.**   However, God also knows our striving and hears our prayers to love more, to grow in compassion, to learn *and do* what He asks. The Bride of Christ will be expected to ***desire*** to be **perfect in her love toward others** by being, applying, developing, teaching, and giving of themselves to others.   When we truly love God, we automatically desire to spurn what is not righteous in the eyes of God. We long to serve God and be with Him for all eternity where love will reign and evil will not exist. But **if we spurn that which God offers us and we ignore what is asked of us we may face the second death in the Lake of Fire** which is a state of existence in a place without God, without righteousness, and devoid of love. It is the final... and forever.... separation of good and evil.

God wants us to be free of evil and to live with Him for all eternity in righteousness and love. He gives us every tool to do so and protects the path we must take to reach that goal. God's love for us is so great that He allowed His Son to sacrifice His life so we could be saved from the captivity of the sin which Satan brings us. Sin dooms us to the Lake of Fire. But God has given us the gift of scripture to help us learn how to avoid the life Satan offers even though we are all sinners. God wants *all* men to be saved and He wants us to succeed. He tells us in Jeremiah 31:3: *The Lord hath appeared of old unto me, saying Yea,* **I have loved thee with an everlasting love:** *therefore with loving kindness have I drawn thee.* And He tells us in Revelation 22:17: *"And the Spirit, and the bride say,* **Come** *and let him that* **heareth** *say, Come, and let him that is athirst come. And* **whosoever will, let him take the water of life freely.***"*

To further implement our understanding, our Heavenly Father has given the angels in heaven the power to inspire every means by which God's message will be brought to **_every_** person who was ever conceived, born or died. Whether through a minister, a friend, a book, a church service or any other venue, God will find a way to reach everyone. On Judgment Day everyone will be clearly reminded of the many times God sent this message to them and when and how it was rebuffed or accepted. **It does not matter what sins we have committed in the past if we now decide to learn of God and follow His precepts.** God forgives us and gladly teaches us. **He teaches us how to take Holy Communion *worthily.*** Under His love and guidance we can grow into those He longs to have with Him forever. The words in Romans 16:20 bring us comfort through the promise: *"And* **the God of peace shall bruise Satan under your feet** *shortly."*

Therefore, we should say as Joshua 24:15 says: *"...As for me and my house, we will serve the Lord".* And while we wait we must... as John 16:33 and Acts 27:25 tell us: *"Be of good cheer".* As we strive to learn and begin to understand the enormity of God's Plan of Salvation, **our faith will continue to grow and we will begin to develop a deeper relationship with God.** Faith is not something which we can see at first but then, when troubles come, we suddenly realize that we have automatically engaged our faith to deal with those concerns. We have brought our troubles to God in prayer and we therefore **no longer feel the anxiety we once felt over similar situations.** We begin to trust that God will take care of us; to trust that **He will bring a blessing out of every situation even when we do not see that blessing right away.... and we also see our anxieties begin to wane.**

Faith is like a muscle.......the more we use it the stronger it gets. Faith is a leap into the unknown... it is offering God something we actually don't have but *want* to give Him. He sees this effort and blesses it. We touch God's heart even more when we trust Him under the most difficult circumstances. God is always faithful to us..... for in 1 John 1:9 the Apostle John teaches: *"If we confess our sins, **he is faithful** and just **to forgive** our sins and **to cleanse** us from all unrighteousness."* Faith in God brings about **the desire to do His will** and thus the desire to love others and help where we can. Faith, coupled with "works", brings us happiness and brings us God's blessing. James 2: 14 tells us: *" **What doth it profit, my brethren, though a man say he hath faith, and have not works?** Can faith save him?"* And in verse 17-18: *"Even so **faith, if it hath not works, is dead**, being alone.......I will show thee **my** faith by **my** works."*

A wonderful analogy about "faith with works" is when we think about someone we love. We "do" things for those we love.... a child might create a drawing for his parents, a minister might visit someone who is bereaved, a neighbor might make chicken soup for a sick friend, a teacher might work diligently to bring knowledge to her students, a husband might purchase flowers for his wife, a parent will teach their children, their family, even their friends about God, a family might always attend church services and pray and tithe. Those are expressions of love, and expressions of some of the "works" which God asks us to do.

We must choose our path ourselves because God has given us each a different talent and thus a different responsibility to use that talent. He has also given us free will and has painstakingly provided every means by which we can learn of His offer. But **it will be entirely up to us to accept.....or not!** Our loving Heavenly Father understands what we face with Satan roaming this earth and attacking those who seek God, thus He provides every means for us to find our way through those attacks. **He will forgive every sin if we have remorse and He will increase what little faith we can muster on our own. No effort on our part will go unnoticed by God.** He loves us unconditionally and suffers when we suffer. But to bring us the future He has outlined, **He is bound by the rules of righteousness.**

Because man fell to sin in the beginning he is destined to remained enslaved by sin **unless** he turns to God...and scripture tells us that **all** men are sinners. Therefore, every one of us is a sinner. Every one of us inherited the tendency to sin. Everyone of us carries sin; **some of which we do not even recognize** until we search God's words and understand His nature. Pride, arrogance, complacency, conceit, *self-justification* and self-aggrandizement are just a few which are often overlooked.

Our lack of understanding causes our Heavenly Father great consternation and is why He leaves no stone unturned to bring us His message and encourage us to learn of Him and trust His ways. *All God asks is that we hear Him out; that we listen to His message* and place it in our hearts. He will work with the little we can do on our own and will **help us recognize the truth in Him and will teach us how to find freedom from sin. But then....we must do our part.**

Faith increases as we build a closer relationship to God. We can assist this process by simply talking to God from our minds and hearts.... not out loud, but in our thoughts. We can speak to God while we work or drive, while we wait or shop, while we cook or dress. We can tell Him our concerns, our hopes and dreams and wishes. We can thank Him for what He has done for us and what He offers us. We can recall the blessings we have received which might be our children, our spouse, our parents, our education, our job, our ministers, our health or when we avoided an accident. These impromptu conversations bring us closer to God and into a real relationship with Him because we are *voluntarily* including Him in everything we think and do.

There is no need to bow our heads or fold our hands when we have these conversations with God....they are distinctly different than our formal prayers. We are simply **speaking to God as we would to our best friend....recounting our joys and sorrows, our hopes and our disappointments, asking for advice and help and thanking Him for His love.** These conversations build our faith and bring us into fellowship with God. Therefore, learning God's Plan of Salvation, learning what God considers sin, learning what the sacraments are and why we need them, entering into prayer and conversation with God, and choosing to follow God's path of righteousness develops our faith and removes our anxieties.

Yes, we will falter, we will fail from time to time, but getting back up, brushing ourselves off and trying again will touch God's heart and help us grow into all God wants us to become. The benefits we will receive from increasing our faith are many; mainly that we can trust that our sins will be forgiven, that we will have a wonderful future in a new world without evil, and that we can live in this current world knowing that God protects us. Hebrews 11:1 tells us: *"Now faith is the substance of things hoped for, the evidence of things not seen."* The words "substance" and "evidence" tell us that those who seek faith will indeed find it.

Bibliography

The Holy Bible, King James Version, published by The New Apostolic Church, Canada, Thomas Nelson, Inc., Camden, NJ, 1972

James Strong, LLD, STD, *Strong's Exhaustive Concordance of the Bible*, Abington, Nashville, thirty fourth printing 1996, copyright 1890

Ray C. Stedman, *Spiritual Warfare*, Word Books, Publisher, Waco, Texas, 1976

Sophy Burnham, *A Book of Angels*, Ballantine Books, New York 1990

Henry H. Halley, *Halley's Bible Handbook,* Zondervan Publishing House, Grand Rapids, Michigan, 24th edition, Copyright 1965

Henry M. Morris, *Many Infallible Proofs*, Moody Press, Chicago, 3rd printing 1977

Henry M. Morris, *The Bible and Modern Science*, Moody Press, Chicago, 1951, 1968

Donald Grey Barnhouse, *The Invisible War,* Zondervan Publishing House, Grand Rapids, Michigan, 12th printing 1976 copyright 1965

Robert Boyd, *Boyd's Bible Handbook*, Eugene, Oregon: Harvest House, 1983

About The Author

Helen Glowacki is an interior designer, writer, teacher, and motivational speaker. She was the host, writer, and producer of the television series "The Contemporary Woman", broadcast by UA Columbia Cablevision. Her writing credentials include an extensive background as a freelance feature and staff writer for four newspapers and for various newsletters and magazines. A graduate of William Paterson University, Helen received a Bachelor of Arts degree, magna cum laude, in Communications. She also received an Associate of Science degree with honors and is a registered nurse. Helen donates her books to cancer centers, drug rehabilitation centers, prisons, youth centers, hospitals, and also to the mission schools of *The Henwood Foundation* and to the Sunday schools in Lahore, Pakistan. Her desire is to use her gift for writing to help others find the love and comforting presence of God. She also emails books to those who are willing to receive testimony or will help in the quest to bring testimony to others. Helen also writes amazing articles based in scripture and filled with insight about how God wants us to conduct our lives. She posts these on Face Book and also on her website so others can use them in their own teaching efforts. Those who have provided reviews of Helen's books tout the beauty of the stories in her novels and many have noted that her non-fiction books are "spiritually uplifting and biblically correct". Her greatest joys are her husband, two children, four grandchildren, and time spent in her New Apostolic faith and in fellowship.

To order additional books, visit the author's website or Amazon.com. To become a distributor of these books, or to purchase in quantity for fund raisers, visit the author's website at: www.helenglowacki.com or email the author at: helen@helenglowacki.com, or visit her personal Face Book page at: http://www.facebook.com/pages/Helenglowacki/ or her book listings on Face Book at: http://www.facebook.com/pages/The-Grandmother-Series/155300907853909?ref=ts

Excerpt from the Tabletop Edition of:

The Story of God's Plan of Salvation

Prologue
Finding The Manuscript

Sarah understood the extraordinary magic of being loved and of loving others. It was like standing on a mountain overlooking a vista of hills and forests or in a valley which wrapped itself around a winding river, or on a cliff overlooking the sea. It was like sitting under a sky filled with twinkling stars hinting at the marvels of the universe; or walking in the shade of old oak trees filled with the happy chatter of birds; or watching a rainbow form, or spotting a field of wildflowers, or hearing the wind whisper through the branches. To Sarah, love was a gift for the heart; soothing and gentling; teaching the soul through its humbling, powerful, demanding mixture of joy and pain. Love was a pathway for growth; the way to change a selfish heart into the giving heart God seeks. Love produces the miracle of a righteous heart. Sarah was grateful for the instruction she received as a child, grateful for what she learned about God. She considered that instruction a great blessing. Today, two days after she and Matt returned from their honeymoon, she would be alone in their home for the first time. She was excited about beginning their life together, about creating personal memories and developing their own life story. She wanted to walk through each room of their home, admire the furnishings which had belonged to Grandma, imagine what their future would provide, and send thoughts to Grandma about how happy she was. With Matt working late, Sarah wanted to read the manuscript they'd found last night in Grandma's desk when Matt placed files into the desk and noticed a sheaf of papers stuck in the back of a drawer. Sarah saw that Matt had found a manuscript, and when she saw the title, her mind filled with wonderful memories of Grandma's story-telling and of Grandma's old Victorian house filled with wonderful clocks. Sarah thought of the chiming and ticking of the clocks, the cedar-smelling armoires, and the oil-scented desk under which she used to hide. Now she was in her own home! As she pulled into the driveway, instead of entering the house through the garage, Sarah decided to enter through the front door just as Grandma had done in her home so she could *listen for the silence.* She wanted to enter the hall, stand very still, *and simply listen* for the quiet... just as Grandma had taught her. Then, she would listen for the ticking of the clocks and in time, for the chimes. The clocks, which Sarah had inherited from Grandma, were hung in every room of the house and Matt had meticulously set them thirty seconds apart so she could enjoy them as Grandma had. So when Sarah inserted the key, pulled the latch, pushed open the door and stepped inside, she stood very still....listening; first for the quiet, and then for the ticking. As she closed her eyes to the quiet, she remembered the times when Grandma had swooped her into her arms, and laid her finger against her lips saying: *"Shhhh."* She remembered imitating what Grandma said and did. Thus Sarah would repeat the word *"Shhhh,"* and she would lay her own little finger against her own tiny lips. They would listen, heads together, ears straining to hear the silence, eyes wide open with anticipation of what was to come.... and after a little while.... Grandma would imitate the ticking sound she heard, saying, *"Tick-tock, tick-tock"* or *"tick-tick, tick-tick"* or *"tick-tock-tock, tick-tock-tock"*. Each clock had a different sound. Thus Sarah learned to listen and to identify the different sounds, and to name which clock made the sound. When the chiming began, she and Grandma would run from room to room to the clock which would chime next. Sometimes Grandma would play a joke on her and switch the clocks between two rooms, and Sarah would run into one room and have to listen again to find the chiming clock... and they would laugh at their great game. Filled with happy memories, Sarah moved from the hall, through the parlour, and into the study. She laid her purse on the console table, placed her briefcase on the floor, and went to their bedroom to change her clothes. Then she went into the kitchen, made a cup of tea and brought it to the study. She curled into Grandma's beautiful wing chair, and began to read the manuscript. After a few paragraphs, memories flooded into her mind of Grandma reading this story to her and her brothers. It had been their favorite bedtime story and had taught them about God's Plan of Salvation. *It helped us so much when life seemed unfair..... I can't wait to share this story with Matt*, she thought. As Sarah began to read in earnest she marveled at Grandma's beautiful handwriting, the script she'd learned as a child. But most of all she marveled at the magnificence and perfection of God's great engineering feat, the physics of the world he'd created just for them through the marvel of His incredibly loving Plan of Salvation.

Chapter One

The Birth of Prayer

Rejoicing in hope, patient in tribulation,

continuing instant in prayer.

Romans 12:12

Once upon a time, in a land of marshmallow clouds and skies of the most beautiful blue, where music played and everyone sang, there lived a multitude of angels who carefully watched the planet below them. The angels were anticipating the progress of the magnificent Plan of Salvation which God had developed for the inhabitants who lived on that planet. The angels felt so blessed because all across the land where they lived, far above the planet below, flowers grew everywhere, and were always blooming, full and perfect... filling the soft, warm breeze with the fragrance of their perfume. The flowers basked under a light so bright that it caused everything to shine vibrantly and enhance the beauty of everything it touched. The clouds were the whitest white imaginable and the grass the greenest green.

The trees were exquisite in their symmetry and beautifully shaped leaves which glowed in graduated colors of gold, green, and rust. An all-encompassing aura of love permeated every living thing and filled the soul with warmth. A great sense of peace and comfort lived in every heart because pure love flowed everywhere in the heavens, and ruled every thought and deed. The angels hoped that someday even those on the planet below would live in such a verdant place of peace and joy. But the spinning planet below the angels was slowly, insidiously dying because it harbored a terrible sickness which was gnawing its way through everything good. None of the inhabitants of the dying planet recognized that their planet was sick or that its life was limited; they thought that everything would always go on as it had in the past. Many had become complacent and selfish and therefore did not recognize what it was that was destroying their planet from the inside, determined to annihilate its goodness and its beauty. The sickness came from evil which fed on anger and envy. The evil was what doomed their planet.

The angels knew that the planet would die, and knew why it would die; even why it had been created, when it was created, and what its replacement would be. This was heaven's secret, and the angels were not allowed to reveal what they knew. They could not share their knowledge with the inhabitants of the planet below them and could not breathe a word about the planet's future unless God told them that they could. They could only watch.... and wait for the completion of God's magnificent plan and sometimes they could offer help. Despite the angels awareness of these dangers they weren't distressed by what they saw because they knew the great future which God had placed into His special plan for the inhabitants who lived there.

They understood the incredible Plan of Salvation which God had engineered, and what the outcome would be. They understood that the inhabitants were in the midst of a great battle between good and evil where the development of pure love in the heart of man was taking place. They knew that love was the only weapon which could overcome the evil which worked to destroy God's creation. They knew that someday the inhabitants must choose between good and evil. Those who chose goodness and made the decision to fight against evil would please God very much. The angels also knew that in Heaven there was a great book made especially for entering the names of the inhabitants who would search for goodness and wanted no part of evil. This book lay open upon a beautiful table made of marble and gold and was very important because it would contain the names of those who God saw as righteous, those who could enter the new heaven and earth which would be free of evil. The word "Lamb" was one of the names for God's Son who was also known as the Lord Jesus, and also known as Christ and it was for Him that God was gathering souls who would come to dwell with Them one day. The great book was called the Lamb's Book of Life because it would contain the names of those who choose to follow Christ; thus those who would reign with Him in heaven when God's plan was completed. Those people would be called the Bride of Christ. To have their names entered into the Lamb's Book of Life, the inhabitants of the cold bleak planet under the heavens would have to learn to love and through that love, overcome evil of their own free will. If the inhabitants did choose goodness and love, they would have to live by God's rules to escape the destruction which would come to their planet, and escape the punishment all evil would face.

God's rules were explained in another Book which God created for the inhabitants. This book was called the Holy Bible. It had been created for the inhabitants so they would have the opportunity to learn exactly what God wanted them to know. The Holy Bible was filled with wisdom, and could teach the inhabitants how to overcome evil by learning how to love. In the pages of this wondrous book were the words of instruction which God provided to help the inhabitants learn of Him, of His love for them, what He wanted to give them, and what would be required of them. This Holy Bible contained everything the inhabitants needed to know about the struggle between good and evil; how evil came into existence, and what would happen to evil when God's plan was completed. Therefore it was important for the inhabitants to use the wisdom found in the pages of The Holy Bible. It would teach them how to overcome evil and what it would mean to have their names written in the Lamb's Book of Life.

God had divided the Holy Bible into sections from which the people could study God's plan and learn how Satan brought harm to the first people God had created whose names were Adam and Eve. It also taught them about the sacrifice of Christ which could redeem the people by freeing them from the captivity which evil brought them. The Bible warned the people about the consequences of allowing evil to become a part of their life and gave them examples of how God placed His Plan of Salvation into the physics of their world to help them. It taught them what God required of those who desired to be a part of His kingdom where no evil would exist. The Bible was a large book containing many smaller books within its covers which described those things which the people needed to understand. The very last of the smaller books was called the book of Revelation and in chapter 21, verse 27, God described the kingdom He hoped the inhabitants could someday occupy and the requirements to do so, saying: *"And there shall in no wise enter into it anything that defileth, neither whatsoever worketh abomination, or maketh a lie, but they which are written in the Lamb's book of life."* Those whose names would be entered in the Lamb's Book of Life were those who would be willing to learn from the Holy Bible, and who would love God and those God loved. As time went on, many inhabitants began to see the difference between good and evil and became thankful for what God was offering them.

When God saw that the inhabitants were thankful for what He provided for them it brought great joy to His heart for this meant that the inhabitants were becoming "different"; they were becoming the "peculiar" people God spoke of in the book in the Bible which was called "Peter". In 1 Peter 2:9 God told them: *"But ye are a chosen generation, a royal priesthood, an holy nation, a peculiar people."* These inhabitants were learning to use that part of their nature which was godly, rather than the part which was selfish when they studied God's words. Their selfish nature left an emptiness in their heart which brought discomfort and sometimes a sense of despair.

They didn't realize that the emptiness came from a lack of love; the pure self-sacrificing kind of love which living by God's words could provide for them. They were learning that filling their heart with love would bring them great satisfaction and joy. The angels who watched the inhabitants on the planet below and waited in patience for them to learn were, in reality, watching God's great and magnificent plan unfold. The plan was called God's Plan of Salvation and had been created by God, the Father; by Christ, the Son of God; and by the Holy Spirit which God sent to dwell in the heart of man to comfort and teach them. When the plan was completed and the Father, the Son, and the Holy Spirit deemed it perfect, God placed His plan into the natural laws of the universe....the physics of His creation....to help the inhabitants learn everything they would need to know. It became an integral part of the universe and was unchangeable; it was righteous and gave everyone the same opportunity for success. It gave every inhabitant the knowledge to choose....of their own free will.....to live with God and all the good He represented.... or with evil. The inhabitants would have to make the choice for themselves: to live under evil or under love.

Thus the great Plan of Salvation for all mankind was built into the natural law of the universe, the physics of the things God placed into His magnificent Creation. It controlled all the elements in the universe and worked for the benefit of mankind both naturally and spiritually. One element of the physics in God's plan allowed the conversations of the inhabitants to reach the heavens. These conversations would be used to measure the development of love in the hearts of the inhabitants, but it would take time for the inhabitants to understand the importance of their conversations and how their words would demonstrate what they learned. At first, they did not know that the natural law of the universe, the physics of things which had been built into God's Plan of Salvation, caused their conversations to be carried to a certain point high above the planet. They did not know that the swirling currents of the breeze grabbed their conversations and brought them to the heavens where they were read then entered into the great heavenly computer and saved. They did not know of, nor understand, this phenomena because they were not yet aware of the wonderful and magnificent plan or the physics of the world which God had developed for them.

Nevertheless, through the natural law of the universe, the physics of things, the conversations of the inhabitants were moved into the love filled atmosphere surrounding the beautiful and verdant land of the angels. When these arrived at the heavens where the angels lived, they were read, recorded and categorized. Most of the conversations were locked into a great computer where they would remain until God's Plan of Salvation was completed. Before its completion, a day of judgment would occur when every inhabitant who had ever lived or ever died would have made their choice between good and evil. The archived conversations would separate what the Holy Bible called the "goats" from the "lambs". Their conversations would be re-played on Judgment Day to demonstrate who had lived righteously and who lived un-righteously.

The Holy Bible explained that the goats would be those who had not chosen to fill their hearts with love and had chosen evil instead. They did not have their names written in the Lamb's Book of Life and therefore would never be allowed to enter God's kingdom. Their conversations, which had been recorded and categorized, would clearly indicate the choices they made throughout their life; the evil they had chosen. This too was a part of the natural law of the universe, the physics of things which God built into His magnificent and loving plan to help in the separation of good and evil. Other conversations would be recognized as very special. Many were directed to God rather than to other inhabitants and so those in the Heavens called them prayers. These prayers blossomed from the thankful hearts of inhabitants who found peace when they spoke to God and expressed their love for Him. These special conversations were also recorded and categorized, but they were separated from the other conversations and sent to the glittering palace which sat high on the majestic mountain.

The palace was where God lived. It was surrounded by a light so beautiful that its multitude of crystal prisms reflected what appeared to be a million rainbows which produced a sparkling tapestry of color across the huge edifice. The palace glowed when God saw that the inhabitants were learning and desiring to place goodness above evil. Because the conversations which were called prayers were considered so special, they were handled with great love. Counterfeit prayers, full of repetition or spoken for show, were easily recognized for their lack of sincerity and saved but not sent to the palace. Only genuine prayers were sent to God's home. Prayers were judged genuine if they came from a pure heart. Only the prayers from a heart which held no guile could pass directly through to the palace.

Counterfeit prayers would be caught and recorded and categorized like the other conversations, but they went only to the great computer. Only pure prayers with no falsity went to the Palace. The Holy Bible taught the inhabitants the value of prayer and what a prayer should contain. If someone prayed just to impress someone rather than to seek an intimate conversation with God, it was not accepted into the Palace. In the book of Luke in the Holy Bible, God warned the people not to pray the way a Pharisee prayed, explaining that the Pharisees exalted themselves and spoke for show and were not sincere. In the Book of Luke, chapter 18, verses 11 and 14, God warned the people that prayers which did not contain love or true thankfulness, were not from a humble heart and would not be accepted. Prayers which did pass to the great palace made the angels happy. They knew these prayers were cherished. They knew that the inhabitants who sent these prayers to God were loved very much by those in the palace.

Most often, these prayers came from those whose names would be written in the Lamb's Book of Life which lay open on the table made of marble and gold and were of utmost importance to those who engineered the natural law of the universe, the physics of things. These prayers always received a response. An immediate response. For God had said of these prayers in the Holy Bible: *"And the publican . . . saying, God be merciful to me a sinner. I tell you, this man went down to his house justified.. . . . he that humbleth himself shall be exalted"* (Luke 18:13-14). The learning process was not difficult for those who had an open heart and a loving nature. But it still took time.

Everyone had to learn the difference between good and evil because Adam had disobeyed God and eaten of the tree of the knowledge of good and evil. 'But God wanted to teach mankind what to watch for and how to avoid the danger of evil and to explain why He wanted to separate good and evil for all eternity. Thus, God planned for every inhabitant to have the opportunity.... and plenty of time..... to learn. God knew that it would take some longer than others, but eventually, everyone would be given the same opportunity and enough time. God worked to show the people who He was and draw them to Him through His love. Those who recognized the loving care God provided to them, changed their prayers to thankfulness and God's heart was touched. He was happy that His plan was beginning to take effect. The natural law of the universe, the physics of things which He had created to protect and teach the inhabitants was progressing and bringing about the development of His peculiar people who recognized the nature of evil, spurned the evil and sought pure love instead. There was singing and rejoicing in the heavens as these new prayers were heard.

The first of God's peculiar people had begun to understand... but even though God provided a response to the prayers of these special people, some did not understand God's response. They had their own ideas about what answer they should receive, and did not accept the response God gave even though it would benefit them in time. It saddened the angels to see an inhabitant lose hope and patience when they received a response they did not expect nor understand. So the angels sometimes whispered comforting words into the ears of the inhabitants, words which God asked them to say. They saw the tears of confusion in some and were moved as they recognized that a pure and seeking heart was looking for a response but could not seem to grasp it. The natural law of the universe, the physics of things, the method by which God had developed and engineered the great and magnificent Plan of Salvation for His people meant that the people would have to learn trust and patience so that someday they could choose who they would trust for all eternity. The angels saw that the prayers of the inhabitants were demonstrating that they were growing in faith because their prayers began to include the words: *"Thy will be done"* and *"I trust in Thee."* This brought joy to the hearts of the angels and to the heart of God. The tears of confusion had done their work and while some chose to walk away from God, others stayed and waited upon His good favor.

The inhabitants who stayed had chosen wisely. The training which the inhabitants were now enduring would come to an end once they were equipped to make their choice between good and evil. Some would move quickly along this path, others slowly, but God gave every inhabitant an opportunity to achieve the goal. Prayer from a pure and seeking heart would lead to trusting God and this trust would lead to the development of a noble heart which could be made worthy to become a part of God's family. Prayer was the very first step toward this goal. In the Holy Bible, in the book of Psalms Chapter 102, verse 1 were written the words: *"Hear my prayer, O Lord, and let my cry come unto thee."* and if the people prayed with their heart, wanting to converse with God, their prayers would go directly to the glittering palace. Thus, through these prayers the inhabitants demonstrated their growth and development.

Progress had been made and God's plan was moving along as intended, with the proof of this evident in the prayers of the inhabitants. Sometimes, however, because evil was not yet bound, many strayed from the pure love and understanding God wanted for them. So God taught them through scripture about a land which represented righteousness and was a place where love could dwell. He also taught them, through the Holy Bible, about another land which represented unrighteousness and was a place which would eventually harm their souls if they chose to live there. So when one of the inhabitants succumbed to the temptations of evil, it was as if he had moved to the land of unrighteousness. When he repented of his sins, it was as if he returned to the land of righteousness where he belonged, where God wanted him to be.

Whenever the inhabitants gave in to the temptations of evil, they slipped back into the land of unrighteousness and sampled the wares evil used to trap them. The angels had a heavy heart because the Father, the Son and the Holy Spirit had engineered the magnificent Plan of Salvation so the birth of pure love could evolve in the hearts of mankind. But, sometimes sadness was the best way to teach mankind to recognize what his choices were and help him understand the difference between good and evil. It was how they would learn that they had free will and that they would be called upon to make a choice between good and evil. When the days ended and the Plan of Salvation was completed it would be too late. God explained in the Holy Bible, in Galatians 6:9, that they would reap the benefits of their godly labor, saying: *"And let us not be weary in well doing: for in due season we shall reap, if we faint not."*

Therefore, many who had strayed from God's direction because of evil, came back; once again seeking His love and His forgiveness, hoping to learn His words and walk in righteousness. These inhabitants learned that living a life away from God and in the midst of evil was not what they wanted for their lives. Thus when any inhabitant of the cold, bleak planet came to repentance and again sought God, the heavens rejoiced; the angels sang; God smiled and the plan moved ahead. It was the learning process which would allow man to recognize that they must make a choice; that no one else could make that choice for them. From these lessons yet another kind of prayer was born in the heart of man and began to reach the heavens. These were prayers which demonstrated what the inhabitants learned when they left the presence of God and what they felt in their hearts when they came back to Him. It demonstrated that the inhabitants now understood that God never left them even though they had left Him. The angels could see that now the people understood the difference between living in the land of righteousness or unrighteousness.

Finally, the lessons of prayer and the heartache of evil were understood by many of the inhabitants. Mistakes were still made, but many stayed faithful to God and valued what they were given. The great and magnificent Plan of Salvation was in effect; and the natural law of the universe, the physics of things, was a miracle to watch as it unfolded and encouraged love to evolve. But then came a day when the inhabitants were tested, and were faced with what they thought was silence from God. They were made to wait for the answer to their prayers so their patience and their faith could be tested. This was to teach the inhabitants to cling stedfastly to the gift of prayer and continue in their trust of their Heavenly Father when evil launched its attack against them. This too was part of God's Plan of Salvation, His desire to help His children.

Sometimes, when the inhabitants had to wait for the answers to their prayers, they asked questions about their lack of understanding, about the timing of the answers to their prayers, and about the feelings and concerns which burdened them. God was glad that His people were conversing openly with Him. He was happy to see them trust Him and expect His help. He was so touched by this that He granted other blessings to His people so they would recognize that He was still with them even if He did not provide immediate answers to the current concerns they voiced in their prayers. The inhabitants came to recognize God's gifts and developed even more love for and trust in their Heavenly Father. Their prayers still went through the test of sincerity, and when they passed this test and traveled to the palace, God listened and understood. Those who chose to wait for God's answers and to trust that He would answer in His time grew in faith. God's heart was moved as the inhabitants told Him that they accepted His will for them no matter what that would be. God smiled, and the heavens sang again with joy, and God rewarded them for their patience and for their unwavering trust.

This had been the lesson of prayer which God gave His children. Now the magnificence of God's great Plan of Salvation could move into the next phase of completion, which was to create within the heart of man a hope for his future, a hope so strong, so deep that it would be unshakable, even when evil came to whisper doubt. Thus, as new prayers rose to heaven and the inhabitants demonstrated the role which prayer now played in their life, they were ready for more. This first step in God's magnificent Plan of Salvation now lived in their hearts and new prayers proved their progress and caused the angels to sing a new song and the heart of God to rejoice. This pleased God and worked a sort of magic on the inhabitants' conversations. They were no longer demanding or accusing; they were loving and appreciative. God could see that His great plan—the plan which He had placed into the natural law of the universe, the physics of things—had successfully completed its first phase. The development of man now had the foundation of prayer to sustain it; the great phenomena of perfect prayer would bring growth and comfort to the souls of the people.

There were other phases of God's Plan of Salvation yet to come which would bring fruition to the process of God choosing a bride for His beloved Son, the Lord Jesus. The Bride would help the Lord Jesus during the thousand-year kingdom of peace when evil would be bound for a time. Only the Father knew the day and the time when He would send His Son back to the Earth to retrieve His Bride. The Bride would be those who had proven themselves by choosing to live by God's statutes. Even God's Son, the Lord Jesus, did not know when God would tell

Him to fetch His Bride. God explained this to His people in the Holy Bible in the book of Matthew chapter 25, verse 13: *"Watch therefore, for ye know neither the day nor the hour wherein the Son of man cometh."* In Matthew 25:21, God explained the reward for faithfulness: *"Well done, thou good and faithful servant; thou hast been faithful over a few things, I will make thee ruler over many things: enter thou into the joy of thy Lord."*

The inhabitants knew from the Holy Bible that there would be a time of great destruction on their planet when God sent His Son to take them to heaven. Thus many heeded God's words, believed them, and followed His statutes. But few fully understood that God had put a magnificent plan into place which would help them ready themselves for that day. Nor did they realize that evil watched them and worked to stop their progress. Now, with prayer established in their hearts, the inhabitants of the cold, bleak planet below the angels were ready for the next step. They would be comforted by the power of prayer as they entered the next learning process in God's Plan of Salvation, the natural law of the universe, the physics of things which God put into place just for them. This next phase of God's plan was to be the development of hope.

"O Lord, Give me Understanding according to thy word."
Psalm 119:169

"Pray without ceasing."
1 Thessalonians 5:17

Available through Amazon.com and from the author's website: www. helenglowacki.com.
English Edition: ISBN: 978-0-9893-8074-4, German Edition: ISBN: 978-0-9893-8073-7 ,
Spanish Edition: ISBN: 978-978-0-9893-8075-1

𝒩ovels

by Helen Glowacki   (Book Size 6 x 9)

When God Broke Grandma's Heart: (208 pages) Rising from sorrow to become a beacon of faith Grandma struggles in an abusive marriage until God moves her from unequally yoked and broken to the healing of His love and forgiveness. Her granddaughter Sarah learns where to find answers to her problems and carries that legacy to those she loves. **Paperback: ISBN 978-0-9847-2110-8**

When God Took Grandma Home: (260 pages) About the heartache of drug addiction, of the enemy who destroys children through drugs, why God allows righteous anger, why we should pray for those in eternity and a description an incredible experience of faith for Matt and Sarah about why God allowed such heartache to occur. **Paperback: ISBN 978-0-49847-2111-5**

When Grandma Chased the Spirits: (208 Pages) The magnetism of idolatry, it's invisible power, and the heartache of bearing a child out of wedlock brings debilitating panic attacks to Mary and affects her husband Kevin. When Matt and Sarah tell them about their faith, God engineers a miracle to solve what that they thought impossible to resolve. **Paperback: ISBN 978-0-9847-2112-2**

The Granddaughter and the Monkey Swing: (284 pages) A wedding, a broken engagement, renovating and decorating a home through Divine Proportion, the truth about Halloween, and the gift of role models create a tender story of friendship. Helping through the planning and problems of a wedding culminates in the unveiling of a secret. **Paperback: ISBN 978-0- 9847-2113-9**

Grandma's Little Book of Poetry: The Story of God's Plan of Salvation: (277 pages) This original version with poems is a beautiful whimsical story for all ages. It begins when Sarah finds a manuscript in Grandma's desk and recognizes the story Grandma read to her and Josh and Caleb when they were children. Angels watch the inhabitants below them struggle to find God. **Paperback: ISBN 978-0-9847-2114-6**

Abiding Faith, Hidden Treasure: (262 pages) Serving in Iraq, Jim loses his faith to see a loving God allow so much heartache. Barbara invites him to dinner where Grandma shows him why creation and evolution co-exist and God's enemy creates the injustices Jim blames on God. Letters from the grave bring an incredible experience of faith. **Paperback: ISBN 978-0-9847-2115-3**

And Then They Asked God: (295 Pages) When Rebecca and Jayden arrive at their college campus they are overwhelmed by betrayal. Losing the values Rebecca once cherished fills her with guilt so monumental that she cannot forgive herself. Chaldeth the evil angel is defeated when God's grace frees Jayden and brings Rebecca's recovery. **Paperback: ISBN 978-0-9847-2116-7**

WHAT IS FAITH?

Caleb's Testimony: (262 pages) Caleb would have taken bets on his ability to trust God explicitly....until his accident.. Now, he and Ann must face the wrath of Satan aimed at causing them to blame God for their misfortune. Can they give up everything they worked for if God asks this of them? **Paperback: ISBN 978-0-9847-2119-1.**

The "Why God Why" Series
by Helen Glowacki   (Book size: 5 ½ x 8 ½)

To What Purpose?: (126 pages) This first book in the *Why God Why* series answers questions about why we are here, what we need to learn, and what God plans for us. It is an excellent book for testimony and one you will share with others. **Paperback: ISBN 978-1-4507-7580-9**

Why God, Why?: (126 pages) This second book in the *Why God Why* Series describes why we experience heartache, its purpose, and how to face it. It answers questions about God's plan for us and what we need to do to be found worthy. **Paperback: ISBN 978-1-4507-7581-6**

Why Trust Scripture?: (126 pages) This third book in the *Why God, Why* Series addresses the challenges against scripture, who wrote the Bible, the importance of the sacraments, what role Satan plays, and how health and the Bible are related. **Paperback: ISBN 978-1-4507-7582-3**

What Should I Know about Life after Death and the Coming Tribulation?: (126 pages) What occurs following death, what will happen during the tribulation, and what the seven seals could mean to us are explained in this fourth book of the series. **Paperback: ISBN 978-1-4507-7583-0**

What Does God Want Me to do Right Now?: (126 pages) A concise explanation of what God asks of us, how we can live up to His expectations what is required to become a part of the Bride of Christ, and what God plans for the future with or without us. **Paperback: ISBN 978-1 4507-9076-5**

Do My Little Sins Really Count? (126 pages) Most of us believe that the little sins don't really matter but scripture explains why they do and teaches is about the seven deadly sins, sin by proxy, and sin by commission and omission which can affect whether or not we take Holy Communion worthily. **Paperback: ISBN: 978-0-9847-2117-7**

What Do Angels Do? (126 pages) Few of us know that there are three levels of heaven in which nine different ranks of angels exist. Nor do they know that these angels have been assigned three very different tasks. This little book takes the

115

mystery out of what angel's do, who rules them, and how they affect our lives. **Paperback: ISBN: 978-0-9847-2118-4**

What is Faith? (126 pages) Faith increases as we increase our understanding of God's Plan for mankind. It is only through learning God's words that we can know what God asks of us and why. It is only through realizing that God is bound by His own rules of righteousness that we can find the key to increasing our faith and helping us become all that God wants us to become. **Paperback: ISBN: 978-0-9893-8076-8**

Coming Soon: Satan's Gift of Fear?

Non-Fiction Books

By Helen Glowacki   (Book Size 5 ½ x 8 ½)

Politically Incorrect: The Get Some Gumption Handbook For When Enough is Enough: (406 pages) Fifty timely and controversial issues are examined under the politically correct approach and compared to what scripture tells us is the approach that God wants His children to take. **Paperback: ISBN 978-1-4507-9074-1**

Overcoming Depression: How To Be Happy: (258 pages) We all face heartache, and all feel sad from time to time. But depression lingers and can result from many different causes. It can rob us of hope and destroy our relationship with God. Thus our Heavenly Father tells us through scripture how we can tap into His blessing and His direction and brings joy out of tribulation. **Paperback: ISBN 978-1-4507-9077-2**

What No One Tells You About Addictions: (216 pages) Discussing the merits of tough love, the selfish co-dependency of the enabler, what scripture tells us about spiritual warfare and invasion, and generational sin, make this book a must read. **Paperback: ISBN 978-1- 4507--9075-8**

"As For Me and My House,

We Will Serve The Lord"

Joshua 24:15

Book Reviews

Reverend (District Apostle Ret.) Richard C. Freund, President of The New Apostolic Church, USA, Sea Cliff, New York: Magnificent writer, a story which makes the reader become emotionally involved, a joy to read, strong Christian values. *"When God Broke Grandma's Heart",* best seller quality.

Reverend (District Apostle Ret.) Richard C. Freund, President of The New Apostolic Church, USA. Helen's new novel, *"When God Took Grandma Home"* "Delights, brings comfort to those who grieve. Inspires, gives insight into the after-life, masterful portrayal.

Reverend Andrew Muliokela: New Apostolic Church in Alexandria, Virginia, formerly from Zambia Africa: *The Granddaughter and the Monkey Swing* and this series of books are awesome! A journey unlike another, I was reading a great novel, learning about confidence, love and support but also learning Bible verses at the same time! Helen Glowacki teaches through her books and I recommend them 100%. You'll enjoy the journey!

Reverend Frederick Rothe, (Ret. New Apostolic Church, New York) Palm Beach Gardens Congregation, Florida: Spent 48 years serving God and another 30 in the congregation. These books contain an accurate account of what God wants of us and why we suffer. The application of scripture and the people in the stories stand for the principles God wants in all of us.

Reverend Kevin Speranza, New Apostolic Church, Palm Beach Gardens, Florida: *And Then They Asked God* so happy I read this, weaves, documents biblical precepts, addresses political correctness, moral & political corruption, biased teaching, insidious growth of socialism renamed progressivism, self-importance, guilt and its debilitating power. WELL DONE! Identifies danger, artfully and Biblically addresses them.

Reverend Luke Jansen, Sr. V. P., Medical Connections, Boca Raton, Florida: "To Ms. Glowacki, author of **The Grandma Series**: grateful for your books, refreshing to find a Christian author who sees the *difference* between religion and spirituality AND that the two can and should be used in the same sentence.

Reverend Derryck Beukes, Montana-De Aar Congregation, Northern Cape, South Africa: Dear Helen, I personally often use your articles in my soul care visits, especially where youth are involved. I can assure you that your articles made a difference to my way of thinking, and I am busy encouraging fellow priests to read your works, as they are so factual and insightful! Thank you for your hard work. I thank God for you, and the wisdom He gave you! Please continue with the excellent work.

Deacon Shadreck Wilima, Overspill Congregation, Ndola, Zambia: Your articles prompt realistic examples which New Apostolic Christians need for their everyday living.

Youth Chairperson, Sunday School Teacher, Mulenga Ernest, Lusaka Central Congregation, Lusaka, Zambia: Through your writing I am constantly reminded of what to be aware of. I pray that God keeps you in the hollow of His hand, guards you and guides you to reach your brethren as you do me. Thanks for caring for the souls of many.

Reverend Aurelio Cerullo, Atripalda Congregation in Campania, Southern Italy: Dear Helen, your books and articles, and social networking bring brothers and sisters the words of our faith and touch the hearts of those who do not know our faith. Our goal is found through the grace of the apostolate and in this sense, the word's from 1 Corinthians 15:58 assumes an important meaning: *"Therefore, my beloved brethren, be steadfast, immovable, always abounding in the work of the Lord, Knowing That your labor is not in vain in the Lord"*. Now that I am a minister of God for about a year I too am grateful to our beloved Father in Heaven for having opened the eyes of my soul, for having removed the plugs from my ears of my heart to hear and listen to His will in connection and communion with those who precede us, guided by the light of the Holy Spirit. God's work always evolves and adapts to the times and even via computers, cell phones and smart phones. I Thank God for having been able to know you, you're a very valuable pearl. God bless you richly.

Rev. Fred Krueger, (Ret.) Lutheran Minister 12 yrs and Clinical Social Worker 26 years, Dallas, Texas: "Inspiring, grabs the heart, author headed to the bestseller list, a pleasure to read, masterful. *"When God Took Grandma Home"* filled with insight into God's plan!

NOTE: The articles which are referred to in these reviews are excerpts from Helen Glowacki's non-fiction books. Not shown are reviews by the ministers who oversee *The Henwood Foundation*'s New Apostolic

Mission Schools in Zambia and review all reading materials prior to distribution.

Edith Stier, wife of a Ret. District Evangelist, Clifton, New Jersey: *The Grandma Series* helps those in need, inspirational, heartwarming, ends with a beautiful example of how God explains our pain, renews hope, shows us the way, creates miracles. I love this series.

Patricia Robinson, wife of a Ret. Rector, Indiana: 5 star rating: *When God Broke Grandma's Heart:* WONDERFUL INSPIRATIONAL NOVEL, enjoyed this book, well written, Bible references, how to achieve peace of mind and soul.

Rosemarie Schaal, wife of an Ret. Reverend, New York: *Abiding Faith, Hidden Treasure:* Reader develops empathy, feels emotion, hears a battle between scientific and spiritual knowledge. Skillful, detailed, brilliant, vivid, teaches that nothing happens that is not planned by Him.

Colette van Loggerenberg, wife of a Minister, Scottsville Congregation of Pietermaritzberg, South Africa: *Grandma's Little Book of Poetry: The Story of God's Plan of Salvation:* This has to be one of the BEST EVER books that I have read....If you ever get the chance to get one of Helen's novels...READ IT. It's like a fairytale but a TRUE fairytale.....Close your eyes and picture this: Grandma with her hair in a bun, glasses perched delicately on her nose, sitting in a rocking chair and her grandchildren sitting on the floor with BIG eyes hanging onto her every word.....but with a twist!!!!! If you have doubts about PRAYER...read this book. I LOVED IT...thank you!

Debbie Espeland, wife of a Rector, Palm Beach Gardens Congregation, Florida: 5 star rating: *When God Took Grandma Home:* HEARTWARMING! This book touched my heart. It is both heartwarming and very spiritual.

Aletta Venter, wife of a Deacon, Scottsville Congregation, Pietermaritzburg, South Africa: *"Grandma's Little Book of Poetry: The Story of God's Plan of Salvation".* What a learning process for me. Oooh I just **love** the way the angels are telling the story, **very original!** When is mankind ever going to learn? The inhabitant's lesson was to learn of good and evil. And they failed miserably each time. The devil has his agenda, and the inhabitants are the target. They call upon God for help, the angels rejoiced. Great....!!!

Aletta Venter, wife of a Deacon, Pietermaritzburg, South Africa: *"Abiding Faith, Hidden Treasure"* is the deepest and most rewarding novel I have ever read, touched my soul, made me cry, author's understanding of God's work is astounding, opens the mysteries

Lisa Mayo, wife of Minister, Palm Beach Gardens Congregation, Florida: Helen's *Why God Why* series of books gave me a new understanding of my faith. They are informative, so enlightening and in-depth, but in a way that is easily understood!!

Tammera Shelton, M.S. Psychology, Odenton, Maryland: I find *"When God Broke Grandma's Heart"* inspirational, beautifully portrays need to let go of negative events and that despite injustice, no pain is for naught.

Robert W. Rothe, USMC 1970-1976, Nevada: 5 star rating: *When God Broke Grandma's Heart:* Outstanding writer, kept me riveted, an angel sent to help through trying days. Thank you for helping me find peace.

Katharina Leipp, Schopfheim, Germany: This is the first time I have ever heard of a female New Apostolic author and I am very impressed by your articles. I have sent your link to my Shepherd and German friends and would like you to consider advertising in our German *Our Family Magazine.*

Claudine Visagie, South Africa: I'm trying to think of a way to introduce Helen's books and articles to others... especially to our youth. They are life changing!

Rebecca Mukuta Mukato, Lusaka, Zambia, Africa: Speaking on behalf of my Dad, District Elder Mukato, your articles are brilliant because they have changed me! Because of your articles my Dad has less headaches!

Robert Henry Parkes, Pietermaritzburg, South Africa: You are gifted with the verses and writings you do and are so inspiring to others. God is really using you as His special servant. You are really a wonderful person and we thank the Lord for you our sister in faith.

Frank Geores, from Port St. Lucie, Florida: *"When Grandma Chased The Spirits:* beautiful spiritual experience, can see caring nature and loving heart of author, eloquently reveals her love for God and search for truth. Worthy of the Star of Bethlehem rating. Thank you for sharing your magnificent gift.

Ben Lodwick, Avid Reader., from Brookfield, Wisconsin: Wow! An eye opener about God's plan of salvation, and why bad things happen to good people. Reminds me of Jim LaHaye and Jerry B. Jenkins "Left Behind Series". MUST READ!"

Dr. Walter Forman From North Palm Beach, Florida: *Grandma's Little Book of Poetry: The Story of God's Plan of Salvation:* a "wonderful book about success and failure in life. All Helen's novels are wonderful, a balm for the soul and an education to the seeker."

Susan Day, From Jupiter, Florida: *Abiding Faith, Hidden Treasure* : I hated to put it down, couldn't wait to pick it up, read all Helen's books, proves every point, shows what to do through God's words. I am 90 and Helen's books have helped me call on God.

Georgette Rothe, From Fort Piece, Florida: *Abiding Faith, Hidden Treasure* was more than I expected; a Biblical course making you re-evaluate your beliefs, enjoyed the journey very much.

Fred D'Alauro, from Palm Beach Shores, Florida: Internet 5 star rating: *When God Took Grandma Home:* Remarkable! Inspirational, moving. Fascinating storyteller with a real message.

Debra Forman, Chester, New York. Internet 5 star rating: *When God Broke Grandma's Heart:* Written from the heart, shares the strong beliefs that shelters us in times of need, courage captivates the reader. Thank you.

Anonymous: Internet 5 star rating: *When God Broke Grandma's Heart:* WHEN LIFE GETS YOU DOWN, PICK THIS BOOK UP, it wrapped its arms around me. A wonderful read. Congratulations on an inspiring work.

A reviewer, a reader in Kentucky: Internet 5 star rating: *When God Broke Grandma's Heart:* Well written, heartwarming, overcoming heartbreak through God, touches your heart. A worthwhile read for all generations.

A reader: Internet 5 star rating: *When God Broke Grandma's Heart:* a must read for all generations. FANTASTIC!

A reviewer Internet 5 star rating: *When God Took Grandma Home:* Moves you, captivating.

A reviewer, a Kentucky reader: Internet 5 star rating: *When God Took Grandma Home:* MUST READ! Touching story of life's tragedies and how lessons learned from these heartbreaking events can turn into blessings.

Characters

in the novels by Helen Glowacki

Grandma: Grandma's life was filled with sibling betrayal and marital abuse. Her love of God, home remedies and famous boxing stance touches the family as she struggles to find her way through heartache.

Sarah: Sarah helps Grandma write her journal, learns about God's plan of salvation and the enemy who wants to harm her. She carries on Grandma's legacy of faith after hearing Grandma's story.

Matt: Matt, Sarah's husband, has a rock-like faith but when he loses a loved one, he struggles with his anger toward God, until he has a miraculous experience of faith.

Paul: Paul is Matt's older brother and a favorite of Grandma's. He is devastated when his wife leaves, but goes on to earn a Captain's license for a seagoing tugboat. His faith sustains him in terrible circumstances.

Mary and Kevin: Mary and Kevin become Matt and Sarah's neighbors and friends. Mary's panic attacks end when God brings them a miracle they never thought possible and Mary gives up her Feng Shui.

Elizabeth: Elizabeth adopts Rebecca, loses her husband twelve years later, is confronted with a potentially deadly illness and searches for Rebecca's birth mother.

Rebecca: Rebecca is Elizabeth daughter and Jayden's friend. Her father's death, the illness her mother faces, and a series of challenges at college almost destroy her.

John: John, a deacon in his church, lost his wife to a debilitating disease, becomes Elizabeth's friend, and helps his daughter Ruth and grandson Jayden through a difficult divorce.

Jayden: Jayden is John's grandson and becomes Rebecca's friend. He has learned that prayer helps solve problems and he and Rebecca begin to share their faith and eventually go off to college together.

Wade and Ruth: Wade is Jim's boss and friend. He adopts two children from Iraq. Ruth is Jayden's mother and John's daughter and she faces a struggle to let go of the past and walk the new path God shows her.

Joshua and Debbie: Fun loving Joshua, Sarah's younger brother, was demanding and judgmental until Caleb stepped in. Debbie looks to Joshua's family to be her role models.

Caleb and Ann: Caleb is Sarah and Josh's older brother. The family looks to him as they once looked to Grandma. Ann, Caleb's wife, the prayer in the family, harbors a secret sadness.

Barbara and Jim: Barbara, Matt's sister is Sarah's close friend. Her husband Jim plays devil's advocate in family debates, and matchmaker for Wade. Jim loses his faith and the family tries to draw him back.

Heza and Bara: Heza and Bara endured a suicide bomber attack when Bara was one and one half years old and Heza as she was born. They are adopted by Wade and brought to the United States.

Chaldeth: Chaldeth is a fallen angel sent to destroy Grandma's family. He plots to bring great heartache to Rebecca and Jayden and their family. His goal is to break their faith.

Durk: Durk, abused by a cruel father, is a sophomore at the college Rebecca and Jayden attend. He brings harm to Rebecca and Jayden, but Jim offers him a second chance.

Professsor T. Nagorra, and Emils, and Dean Peerca: These tenured professors befriend Durk and engage in activities which harm the students and the college campus.

Professors Doog and Sendnik, and President Legna: These three college professors share a faith in God, a love for their country, and a desire to be role models. They help save the campus.

Richard and Rachel: Richard is a physician for whom Caleb built a house on the property next door to where he and Ann. live. Both couples share godly values and thus became friends.

Joe and Preacher: Both men work for the company which hired Caleb to supervise the construction of a shopping mall. Preacher is always trying to teach Joe what scripture says. Joe resists to tease Preacher.

www.ingramcontent.com/pod-product-compliance
Lightning Source LLC
LaVergne TN
LVHW011207080426
835508LV00007B/648